TILL
DEBT
DO US PART

TILL
DEBT
DO US PART

Balancing finances, feelings, and family

Dr. Bernard E. Poduska

SHADOW
MOUNTAIN

Salt Lake City, Utah

Cover illustration by Randall Pixton and Doug Fakkel.

Major portions of the present work were revised from *For Love and Money: How to Share the Same Checkbook and Still Love Each Other,* Salt Lake City, Utah: Deseret Book Company, ©1995.

Library of Congress Cataloging-in-Publication Data

Poduska, Bernard E.
     Till debt do us part
        p. cm.
     Includes bibliographical references and index.
     ISBN 1-57345-587-3 (pbk.)
        1. Finance, Personal. 2. Debt. I. Title.

  IIG179.P555424 2000
  332.024--dc21   00-022314

Printed in the United States of America   72082-6558

10 9   8   7   6   5   4   3   2   1

*To all those whose work
is tangible evidence of
their love for others*

CONTENTS

PREFACE

The saying "until *debt* do us part" seems to reflect today's marital realities more accurately than does the traditional vow "for better or worse." One of the most familiar challenges facing couples and families alike is how to successfully combine their *finances, feelings,* and *family relationships.*

Traditionally, couples have viewed finances separately from relationships and have managed them with pencils, checkbooks, and calculators. But "number crunching" can tell you only where the money has gone; it cannot tell you why it has gone. For instance, the numbers may tell you that you went in the hole $200 last month; they don't tell you that you spent the extra $200 because you were depressed. Numbers can't tell you that you are heading for bankruptcy because your spouse can't control the credit cards, or because you feel inadequate and are trying to keep up with the Joneses, or because you feel guilty about the divorce and don't want the kids to suffer.

Likewise, the most practical computer-generated budget in the world won't last a month if the person who created it failed to consider the needs and feelings of those who are asked to live with it. Frustrations are voiced in such statements as "Was I supposed to go barefoot the rest of the month? I needed a new pair of shoes, and I was tired of doing without just so you could balance your budget," or "It's my money, I worked hard for it, and I've got the right to spend it any way I please."

Clearly, finances and relationships are interrelated, and only by looking at their relationship can a family establish a successful financial management program. To help families meet their financial challenges, this book—organized into three parts—explores financial principles, personality characteristics, and family types.

Part One looks at the way various elements, such as "families of origin" and personality characteristics, affect the way you manage your finances and relationships. Part Two teaches you how to cope effectively with issues, such as debt management and goal setting, that influence your financial past, present, and future. Part Three helps you integrate information from Part One and Part Two in dealing with specific family types and stages in life.

Ten principles depicting the interaction among finances, feelings, and family relationships show how the interplay of these three factors affect the quality of your life. For example, with the understanding that *most financial problems are not money problems but behavior problems,* you will be able to (1) understand why finances play such a crucial role in almost all relationships, (2) reduce or eliminate many financial management problems, and (3) establish a financial management program that provides for your needs and for your loved ones' needs.

A guide to finances and relationships must not only provide sound principles but also show how these principles can be applied. Numerous exercises, case illustrations, examples, and worksheets throughout the book provide practical means of applying principles to everyday situations.

Most people are quite capable of putting their financial lives in order if they can gain enough insight into what is causing their problems, and if they are given the skills to make necessary changes. This book is written for those just starting out in marriage, and for those who have been married for some time but are still struggling with family finances. But most of all, this book is designed to help everyone who wants to manage finances more effectively while enhancing the quality of personal and family relationships.

PART 1

Finances, Feelings, and Family Relationships

Most families have difficulty managing finances because they focus on *numbers* rather than on *people*. They see budgets as a means of accumulating *things* rather than as a means of experiencing *feelings* or enhancing *relationships*.

Finances, feelings, and family relationships are *all* essential elements in a successful financial program. Realizing this and giving each element equal consideration are the first steps toward creating a family financial management plan that focuses on people as well as on numbers.

CHAPTER 1

FINANCIAL PRINCIPLES AND VALUES

"For crying out loud," the irate husband shouted, "money doesn't grow on trees."

"It wouldn't matter if it did," his wife shot back, "because you're sure no Johnny Appleseed."

As the couple's marriage counselor, I quickly stepped in before their verbal attacks could escalate. This kind of exchange was not something new for these two. They had been arguing about money ever since their wedding day.

Finding satisfaction in the way finances, feelings, and family relationships work together in your marriage depends a great deal on how your expectations about each component match your actual circumstances. Most marriage and family counselors are well aware of the interplay between a couple's finances and marital happiness. They find that many of today's couples are ill prepared to cope effectively with both the emotional *and* financial stresses of marriage.

You don't have to be a marriage counselor to know that today's marriages experience far more stress than marriages in previous generations. The traditional family with the wife at home and the husband acting as the sole breadwinner is no longer the norm. Dual-income, dual-career, blended, and single-parent families have replaced the conventional family. Each of these more modern versions has made its own unique contributions to the challenges faced by today's families. As a result, we have a generation that is often thoroughly confused and exasperated over what to expect in financial and marital relationships.

As the complexity of relationships has increased, the complexity of interactions between money and relationships has also increased. For instance, changes in society's attitudes toward married women working outside the home have changed the financial organization of today's families. During the 1950s only one in four American mothers worked outside of the home; this figure grew to three out of four by the mid-1990s.[1]

One of the consequences of this change is that many women no longer depend on men for their financial well-being. Work availability for women has not only increased the degree of independence they experience within marriage but has also increased their freedom to decide *not* to be married. Since today's women are quite capable of supporting themselves, the reasons for getting and staying married have been altered. Many women no longer need to feel "trapped" in marriage, and their status in the community is not necessarily described by their husband's success. Their identity, as well as their credit ratings, can be distinct and independent of their husband's.

On the other hand, many men no longer believe that they can support a family on their income alone. As a consequence, today's couples need to be able to work out misunderstandings and disagreements over finances if they are to have any hope of preserving their relationships.

Couples argue more about financial problems than any other area in their marriage. Surveys conducted by the American Bar Association and other groups indicate that money problems have been a chronic source of difficulty in marriage for decades, and many lawyers believe that financial problems are the leading cause of divorce.[2]

Arguments over money matters occur often in marriages because feelings associated with finances tend to intensify as the number of people involved increases. How effectively a couple can combine the financial and emotional elements of their relationship depends primarily on their ability to establish a sense of balance among the three essential elements of successful family financial management: *finances, feelings,* and *family relationships.*

Finances, Feelings, and Family Relationships

The degree of balance marriage partners achieve among finances, feelings, and relationships depends a great deal on how much of a difference they experience between what they *expect* from each of these three components and what they actually receive.

Finances

How much income you expect each partner to provide and how each of you expects to spend the income is the basis for all ensuing discussions about financial matters. And while dollar amounts alone may look good on paper, a mutually satisfying financial management plan must also consider the feelings associated with the dollar amounts.

Feelings

We seldom spend money just to obtain things. Rather, we spend to experience the feelings associated with the things. Therefore, merely having more money does not necessarily guarantee having more happiness. How effectively we *exchange* the money we have determines whether we are happy. Regardless of how much money we have to spend on a car, for example, if the car turns out to be a "lemon," we are not going to feel very happy.

You exchange money to experience feelings of happiness, love, security, power, pride, and so on. Feelings are the emotional overtones associated with a thought, event, or item, and are more related to what something represents *to you* than with how it may be defined in a dictionary. For instance, the dollar amount you owe to a relative may be smaller than many of your other bills, but the feelings you associate with *that* particular debt may make you disregard the practicality of first paying off larger, higher interest loans. Conversely, the actual cost of a single rose may not be all that great, but what the rose represents and the feelings associated with it can be priceless.

As a consequence, when dealing with family finances, it is far more critical to ask how your partner *feels* about a purchase than to merely ask how much something costs. "How would you feel if I were to spend _____ on _____?" places the top priority on your partner's feelings, whereas asking "How much will it cost?" or "Can we afford it?" places the emphasis on the object. When you do not consider your partner's feelings, you may discover that the true cost of an item may far exceed its purchase price. If a purchase creates distance and resentment in the relationship, you may be hard pressed to derive any lasting happiness from owning it.

An irate wife, whose feelings are not considered when her husband buys himself some new hang-gliding equipment, may express her feelings in no uncertain terms.

"No," she says, "I do not want to see your hang glider. Nor do I want to watch you hang glide, or talk to your friends about hang gliding, or have anything else to do with hang gliding. That money was supposed to be used for a family vacation this summer, not to satisfy your need to fly with condors."

As an equal partner in a relationship that involves finances, you have the right to expect your spouse to consider your feelings in financial decision making. The final decision may not always be the one you hope for, but if your feelings are considered, you can more easily support the decision, and your relationship will be more easily preserved.

Family Relationships

Your relationships with members of your family reflect (1) the degree of commitment you have to them, (2) the degree of understanding you have about their needs, (3) the amount of flexibility you are willing to exercise to satisfy those needs, and (4) the relative importance, or priority, you place on their general welfare. In a marital relationship, you have the obligation to dedicate yourself to these responsibilities and every right to expect your spouse to do the same.

To many, the interdependency among finances, feelings, and family relationships is self-evident and confirmed in countless incidents of caring thoughtfulness, giving and taking, misunderstandings, and hurt feelings. This interdependency shows up in situations that are as complex as getting remarried:

"Ralph called to let us know that he won't be able to make his child-support payment this month," Martha said with a disgruntled sigh, "so I guess we'll have to use some of your paycheck for the rent."

"But if we use some of my pay for the rent," her husband protested, "there won't be enough left for me to make *my* child-support payment."

It can also show up in something as simple as buying Christmas gifts ("How come we only spent $23 on *my* mother's gift and over $120 on *your* mother's gift?"), paying bills ("Didn't we agree to use the credit cards only for emergencies? What's this Visa bill for $89?"), or maintaining a car ("You can take the bus, ride a bicycle, or even walk for all I care, but I'm not going to put another penny into that car of yours. Didn't I tell you not to buy it in the first place?").

Ten Financial Principles

To help you develop a financial management plan that will work for you, here are ten principles that provide a broad guide to financial thinking and behavior. By giving these principles thoughtful consideration, you may gain some insight into why you have been plagued with financial difficulties and how you may finally be able get out, and stay out, of debt.

Many financial principles can be understood only through years of study and experience, yet some are founded on simple common sense and are easy to understand. These can be expressed in the form of *maxims*—short, popular sayings that embody some familiar truth or useful thought: "You should risk no more than you can afford to lose." Founded on practical life experiences, maxims serve as rules of conduct. The following ten can stimulate thinking about basic financial management decisions.

Principle 1: Financial problems are usually behavior problems rather than money problems.

Many people believe that they *deserve* a particular standard of living and that if they could just make more money, they wouldn't have financial problems. But in most cases, making more money just adds zeroes to old deficits—instead of owing $1,000, you owe $10,000 or $100,000. The Morris family, for example, earns $40,000 a year but spends $45,000. The Palmer family also earns $40,000 a year but spends only $35,000. The Morris family is going into debt at the rate of $5,000 a year, while the Palmer family is relatively rich with $5,000 a year left over. The difference between the families may be due to the fact that the Morris family is a young family trying to accumulate needed assets (washer and dryer, furniture, and so on), while the Palmer family is more established and has already acquired many of the basic items considered to be indispensable. However, when two families are essentially equal, differences in their financial status are due to behavior.

Similarly, it is not enough to merely calculate how much you owe to determine what steps you must take to rectify your current financial difficulties; you must also examine the kinds of behavior that created your debt.

For example, Manuel and Marta earned $29,000 last year and owe $12,000. Stan and Kristi also earned $29,000 last year and also owe $12,000. Although these two couples appear to be quite similar, major behavioral differences led to their indebtedness. Manuel and Marta's debt resulted from a medical emergency and a lack of adequate insurance. Stan and Kristi's debt, however, resulted from Stan's impulsive purchase of a powerboat that caught his interest at a sports show. Marta worries about Manuel working a second job to pay off the hospital bill; Kristi worries about having to sell one of the family cars to pay off the boat.

Principle 2: If you continue doing what you have been doing, you will continue getting what you have been getting.

If you continue to spend instead of save, you will continue to live from paycheck to paycheck. If you continue to borrow money to get out of debt, you will continue to go deeper into debt. If you continue to use your credit cards impulsively, you will continue to pay high interest rates.

For example, Mr. Anderson explained to his wife how fortunate they were that the new credit card had arrived in the mail. "Look, we can use the $2,000 cash advance on the new credit card to make the back payments on the mortgage. Then we can refinance the car to make the payments on our other credit cards—they're all at their limits, you know. Then we will only have the consolidated loan payments to worry about, and I think I can borrow enough from your parents to make that payment." Unfortunately, this thinking pattern is fairly typical of the way today's families are trying to manage their finances.

Principle 3: Nothing (no thing) is worth risking the relationship.

One definition of a prenuptial agreement is "a contract between two people who love things more than they love each other." This is not to say that we ignore financial considerations before marriage; but we hope these considerations are motivated more by a concern with practical financial management than by a lack of trust.

The word *trust* means the ability to be comfortable while being vulnerable. Trust is an essential element in any successful financial or interpersonal relationship. When couples lack of trust, they may feel safer becoming emotionally involved with things than with people. But one of the quickest ways to destroy a marriage, or any other relationship, is to allow a *love of things* to become a higher priority than a *love of each other*. In the beginning of a relationship, being in each other's presence seems to be enough. Newlyweds even joke about "living on love." Unfortunately, as time passes, complaints and accusations creep into communication patterns: "I can't live like this any more. How can you expect us to get anywhere on what you bring home?" or "I'm tired of scrimping. I deserve something that *I* want once in a while. We always seem to have enough money for the things *you* want, but never for the things *I* want."

A few years ago two young people came to me for marriage counseling. They had been married for three years but complained of feeling distant from each other. "We can be in the same room but we never feel like we're together," the wife lamented. Her husband added, "We feel more like roommates than husband and wife."

As I began to explore their marital relationship, the couple revealed that, even after three years of marriage, the wife still had *her* car in *her* name, and the husband still had *his* savings account in *his* name. When I asked why they had handled their resources this way, the wife answered, "I wasn't sure the marriage would last, and if it didn't, I didn't want to risk losing my car." The husband explained how his first wife had cleaned out their bank accounts before telling him that she had filed for a divorce. Then he shrugged his shoulders, and said, "If things didn't work out in this marriage, I didn't want the same thing to happen again."

Principle 4: Money spent on things you value usually leads to a feeling of satisfaction and accomplishment. Money spent on things you do not value usually leads to a feeling of frustration and futility.

If you know what your values are, you will focus your resources on goals that reflect those values. If you are still not sure what is important to you, you will tend to scatter your resources on a variety of targets, hoping that at least some pay off.

The Turners valued the welfare and happiness of their children above all else, and they smiled at each other as they sat on the lawn watching the children play on a new jungle-gym swing set. The children were laughing and shouting gleefully as they tried out each part of their new equipment. The swing set had cost a lot of money compared to the size of the Turners' income, but it was well worth the price.

The Pavlovics loved music. Both had grown up in musically inclined families. However, they had not gone to a live symphony in over a year. They just could not afford such "luxuries," because payments for their new car were burying them. They blamed social pressure for encouraging them to buy the car. Before moving into an expensive neighborhood, neither of them had even been interested in cars. Taking the bus had been just fine. At least they had been able to ride it to the symphony.

Principle 5: We know the price of everything and the value of nothing.

Unfortunately, the maxim expressed in Principle 5 seems to be all too true in today's world. Because of social pressures and advertising, you may end up buying what you think you *should* want rather than what you *really* want. If this is true of you, you may find it difficult to set your priorities, focus your energy, and define your purpose.

Perhaps you remember wanting to buy something important but had to conclude that you couldn't afford it. Why? Because you already spent the money on something else. For example, as a couple you'd like to answer your church's call for a sizeable charitable contribution. But with payments on the new car, the room addition, recarpeting, and the satellite dish that goes with the new home entertainment center, you just can't afford it. Of course, if you had not allocated money to these other things, you probably could afford it. Actually, you have enough money—you've just committed it to other things.

One of the more common side effects of not being able to afford one thing is that you then substitute something else that may not mean as much to you. For example, if a trip to the Caribbean is not affordable at $4,500, you may substitute a trip to Disneyland at $1,500. The following year you find once again that you can't afford the Caribbean trip, so you go to Disneyland once more. In fact, you end up taking your second-choice trip three years in a row at $1,500 a trip—which ended up costing you $4,500—because you thought you couldn't afford the trip you really wanted. Are you spending your hard-earned money on what you *really* want, or are you substituting?

If you believe that substitution is playing too big a part in your life, then the following principle is worth posting on your refrigerator, writing on the cover of your checkbook, or taping to your credit cards.

Principle 6: You can never get enough of what you don't need, because what you don't need can never satisfy you.

This principle, of course, applies to many areas of our lives. For example, if you need *respect* but try to satisfy this need with power, then you will remain unsatisfied no matter how much power you get. If you need a feeling of *self-confidence* and try to obtain that feeling by using drugs or alcohol, you will never be able to get enough of the addictive substance. If you need *love* but try to satisfy this need with sex, then no amount of sex will ever satisfy you. Nor will you ever earn enough money to satisfy your need for love. If what you need is more *time* with someone, then no matter how many gifts that person gives you, the gifts will never satisfy your need to share memorable moments. What you don't need will never satisfy you.

Carol's situation provides an effective illustration of this principle. Carol is extremely successful in her career. Unfortunately, her job demands long hours and frequent travel. Kimberly, age seven, is watching her mom hurriedly pack a suitcase. "Are you going to be gone very long this time?" she asks softly.

Preoccupied, Carol replies, "Unless something unexpected comes up, this should be a quick one. Two, maybe three days."

Kimberly's lower lip seems to stick out a little farther as she watches her mother pack. Finally she asks rather nonchalantly, "Then you won't be here to watch me dance, will you?"

Carol looks up quickly from her packing and, with a pained

expression on her face, responds, "That's Friday night, isn't it? And Mommy's not going to be able to be there. I'm really sorry, Kimberly, but there's just nothing Mommy can do to get out of this trip. But I promise you—cross my heart—I'll be there the next time you dance. Okay?"

Kimberly looks down at the floor and mumbles, "Okay. I understand."

Not completely convinced that Kimberly accepts the situation, Carol adds, "How about if I buy you something really special while I'm gone? And I mean something *really* special—something that will surprise even you. How would that be?"

Kimberly shrugs her shoulders and sighs, "I suppose it'd be all right."

After reading this case, you may want to ask yourself if your needs and the needs of those you love are really being met. Giving more time and attention to your family members would probably make them happier than they would be if you were to shower them with gifts.

Principle 7: Financial freedom is more often the result of decreased spending than of increased income.

Having financial freedom is not the same as being financially independent. Financial independence implies having accumulated enough wealth to sustain a high standard of living without further effort on your part; financial freedom implies having enough discretionary income to enable you to select a number of alternatives on which to spend your money rather than having to face financial ultimatums. With financial freedom, you can choose to go to the movies *and* go out to dinner, or to pay off both the Visa *and* the MasterCard, rather than choosing whether to heat *or* eat this month.

Just as it is more difficult to *earn* your way out of debt, it is more difficult to *earn* your way to financial freedom. Cutting back on expenses, choosing the less expensive alternative when possible, and using your talents and ingenuity instead of your checkbook will prove the validity of Poor Richard's proverb: "A penny saved is a penny earned."

Although Phil and Mendy were already trying to live by this proverb, their money still seemed to just "disappear" with not a lot to show for it. After paying the monthly bills, and once again having almost nothing left to live on, they decided to cut back on just about everything in an attempt to bring their budget under control. They rode the bus to work and school instead of driving ($100 normally spent on gas per month – $40 bus fare = $60 savings); they went to $1.50 discount movies instead of $7 movies (a savings of $22 each month for every two movies seen); they bought two inexpensive steaks and had a candlelight dinner at home instead of going to a restaurant (savings = $25); they wore sweaters at home instead of turning up the thermostat (savings = $15 per month); Phil took brown-bag lunches instead of eating out (savings = $50); Mendy wrote letters instead of making long-distance calls (savings = $20); and Phil bought a secondhand tool instead of a new one (savings = $15). Their efforts resulted in a $207 reduction in expenditures when compared to the amount they normally budgeted for such items. Keep in mind that they would have had to earn around $325 extra per month (an additional $4,000 per year) to clear the $205 after payroll withholdings.

Mendy and Phil achieved financial freedom by reducing their spending rather than increasing their income.

Principle 8: Be grateful for what you have.

The need for more money to purchase more things can become an endless, futile quest unless you come to grips with who you are and what you really want out of life. We Americans are among the few people on earth who have so much "stuff" that we have to rent storage units so we have some place to put it all. And still we want more.

Begin appreciating what you already have rather than worrying about what you don't have. Even a crummy job can feel (and certainly *pay*) better than no job at all; renting a small apartment sure beats being homeless; and eating leftovers is preferable to going hungry.

Karen and Russ provide a good example of such gratitude. They were married college students living in off-campus housing. Both worked part time, but tuition, books, rent, and utilities took most of what they earned. Food became a luxury. Russ chuckled as he held up a couple of boxes for Karen to evaluate.

"Would Madam prefer macaroni and cheese or a selection from our delicious assortment of Top Ramen?"

Karen, assuming an aristocratic pose and a highborn tone of voice, replied, "I do believe I'll partake of the macaroni and cheese, with, I might add, a hot dog, medium well. Thank you."

Trying not to smile too broadly, Russ continued, "And would Madam care for dessert? We have an excellent vanilla ice cream."

Karen looked up in surprise, dropping her aristocratic pose. Grabbing Russ's arm, she asked, "We've got ice cream? You're not kidding me, are you? We really have ice cream? Where'd we get the money to buy ice cream?"

"Tom had to study for an exam, so he gave me a couple of bucks to run a computer program for him. I decided we deserve a treat at least once in a while."

Principle 9: The best things in life are free.

As the old song says, "The best things in life are free"—and they are even better when you share them with those you love. If you have gone through hard financial times with someone special, you know the importance of thoughtful gestures and creative humor in trying to make do.

For entertainment, one couple liked to go to a local mall to see if each partner could "spend" $10,000 in less than an hour on things they really wanted. Of course, they didn't really have $20,000 to spend, but they had fun picking out expensive watches, strange-looking sweaters, and oversized pictures. It didn't cost them a cent, and it was fun—most of the time.

Making do can often provide opportunities for personal growth. For example, one night Seiko, looking out the kitchen window, commented that the storm seemed to be getting worse. Dinner was almost on the table and everyone was about to sit down when the electricity went out. A few of the younger children cried out but were immediately calmed by one of the older children. Their mother began groping in one of the cupboards and in a calm voice said, "Everyone just stay put for a minute. I know there's a candle around here someplace. Aha! Found one. Anyone for a candlelight dinner?" By then the children were feeling the adventure of the occasion, and one offered to be the waiter.

After dinner, they all helped build a fire in the fireplace and took turns reading their favorite nursery rhymes. Some were curled up in blankets and starting to drift off when the electricity came back on and the magic of the moment disappeared in the glare of the ceiling light. In unison they all bemoaned being called back to the twentieth century.

Principle 10: The value of individuals should never be equated with their net worth.

Each individual in a family is unique, one of a kind, and therefore irreplaceable. Some individuals may contribute humor, others may contribute music. One person may provide the family with emotional stability while another may provide financial stability. But the worth of an individual can never be assessed in dollars.

Imagine attending a funeral service in which the eulogy stated, "Frank wasn't worth very much. After all of the expenses of this funeral are deducted, I doubt if his net worth will exceed $10,000. Unfortunately, Frank was struck down in the prime of his consuming. He didn't have enough time to really accumulate much. All of us who were close to Frank knew there were a lot more things he wanted to buy. With a little more purchasing time, he could have really amounted to something."

We are remembered not for what we consume but for our contributions and for the difference we make in the lives of others. Our net worth reflects our financial status; our contributions to the welfare of others reflect our personal worth.

Personal Values

Are you spending your time and money on what you really value, or are you merely disbursing them by *default?* Lacking self-knowledge and merely reacting to whatever comes our way, we often live our lives by default. A life led *by design,* however, is one in which the consequences reflect thoughtful planning, dedication, and a sure knowledge of our values.

Values are relatively permanent beliefs about what you regard as desirable, worthy, or right. Values tend to reflect upbringing and change very little over a lifetime. Your values help determine the relative importance you place on such situations as saving your marriage, getting a good education, or getting out of debt. They give your life meaning and purpose. As you attempt to develop a sound financial plan, it is essential that you decide which of your values are most important to you.

Replaceables and Irreplaceables

Someone once said, "Values are reflected in how well a person is able to distinguish between what is replaceable and what is irreplaceable." For many, it has become increasingly difficult to make this distinction, and they tend to devote more of their resources to obtaining things that are replaceable than to preserving what is irreplaceable. They may also fail to receive any personal satisfaction from their possessions or to see any intrinsic value in them. Such people are unable to meaningfully connect with the world around them.

A replaceable thing is usually seen as having utilitarian value only. It is prized only as long as it serves some purpose; once that purpose has been achieved, it is discarded. Something that is not one of a kind is usually considered *replaceable*. Something with an intrinsic, personal value, or something that is one of a kind is usually considered *irreplaceable*. Car fenders, screen doors, most jobs, and money are replaceable; great pieces of art are irreplaceable. Most toys are replaceable; favorite blankets, dolls, or teddy bears are irreplaceable. Most jewelry is replaceable, but great-grandmother's wedding ring is irreplaceable. Most things built by others are likely to be replaceable, but what we and our loved ones create with our own hands and hearts often becomes irreplaceable. Individuals are unique and therefore irreplaceable. Relationships that have taken a great deal of time and effort to build are also irreplaceable.

Irreplaceables—whether things or relationships—represent something you value, something that justifies hard work or sacrifice, something that provides feelings of gratification, a sense of purpose, or meaning to life.

The Values Inventory

Unfortunately, it is not uncommon to put forth a great deal of hard work to get something you value, such as an adequate income, and then waste it because you have not created a budget that reflects your priorities or considers what you really value. Since you naturally want your resources to go toward what is important to you, a difference in values among family members can easily lead to conflicts over how family resources should be spent. While family members will seldom reach total agreement on all issues, a sense of fairness is more likely to prevail if all involved feel that their values receive equal consideration. Serious problems arise when the family fails to discuss significant differences.

The Values Inventory, Worksheet 1.1 (pages 22–23), invites you to examine your values and compare them with your spouse's values. Each of you fill out one of the two copies of the worksheet provided at the end of this chapter. After you have completed your worksheets, first share your personal responses to the values, then compare how you each thought the other would respond to a particular value.

Value Conflicts

Communication in this area is essential. Even if you have a fairly good grasp of your values, you may be unable to communicate them effectively to loved ones. As a result, you silently watch as your spouse spends money on everything but what you want it spent on. When things finally come to a head, you tell your spouse—perhaps in anger—how you really feel. Surprised, your spouse responds, "If you had told me how important it was to you, we would have bought it." Still hurt, you counter, "If you really loved me, you'd have known how important it was to me." Lack of love, however, is not the problem. The problem is lack of communication.

Meaningful Units

One way to communicate the relative value you place on things is to convert them into *meaningful units*. A meaningful unit represents something that (1) you value, (2) you know the cost of in effort or labor, and (3) you know, in its absence, causes discomfort and inconvenience. A meaningful unit, for example, might be a dinner out (something you value), a car (something you work hard to obtain), or a telephone (something that is inconvenient to be without). Almost anything you value in some way can be termed as a meaningful unit.

Once you have determined what represents a "meaningful unit" to you, you can compare it with other "meaningful units" valued by others. This is called finding the "relative value" of an item—the amount of value an item has in relation to other items.

Meaningful units can help you compare the value of less expensive items to the value of more expensive items. For example, to Norma a $35 pair of children's shoes is a meaningful unit. She uses that to compare the relative value of other financial demands, such as her husband's desire to spend $348 on a new shotgun. Norma calculates that she could buy approximately ten pairs of shoes for the children with the amount of money her husband wants to spend on a shotgun. To Norma, the relative value of a new shotgun represents, in meaningful units, ten pairs of shoes.

You can arrive at the relative value of each of your financial demands by calculating how many of your own meaningful units could be bought for the cost of a particular demand. Meaningful units can also be used the other way around, comparing the value of more expensive items to less expensive items. For example, you may discover that you could have bought a plane ticket and visited Grandma in person (meaningful unit) for the amount of money you spent on last month's long-distance phone calls. You might also find that you could have bought those much-needed tires with what you spent on fast food last month.

It is helpful to compare your meaningful units with your partner's. For example, what you spent on renting videos (your meaningful unit) in the past two months could have paid for dinner at a nice restaurant (your partner's meaningful unit). By making such comparisons, you will be able to better understand each other's value system and work together in establishing spending priorities.

Attitudes

In any relationship, questions about how to allocate resources arise. "Should the money go to mortgage payments or car repairs? To charities or home improvement projects?" Arguments often result from a difference in values. In most cases, however, couples find that they have similar *values* but different *attitudes.*

An attitude is a state of mind based on your opinions and judgments about the world around you. Your attitudes can be optimistic or pessimistic, favorable or unfavorable, charitable or hostile. They reflect a position you have taken because of your values, and therefore they are much more flexible than values. For example, you and your spouse may both value education, but your attitude is that private schools are the way to go, while your spouse thinks public schools are quite sufficient. Related disagreements, therefore, result from differing attitudes rather than differing values.

As this example illustrates, attitudes can have a major impact on family finances. A decision to send the children to private rather than public schools would greatly increase family educational costs. Saving money for education, therefore, would need to be a financial goal (see chapter 8).

Goal Conflicts

Whenever you are in a situation that demands a decision between two alternatives or goals, you will experience the stress associated with conflict. The things you like about a goal are desirable and attract you, while the things you don't like about a goal are undesirable and tend to push you away. Most of life's decisions come with one of three combinations of these two qualities.

The first combination arises when you are forced to choose between two goals that are both desirable. This dilemma is aptly described in the familiar cliché "You want to have your cake and eat it too." For example, say you are trying to decide between buying a long-wanted new computer or spending money on badly needed home repairs. Both goals are desireable, but both will remain blocked until you make a decision. Your feelings of frustration, stress, and anxiety will continue until you do. Eventually, you may base your decision on emotional relief rather than on a well-considered process of elimination.

When dealing with any conflict, you must keep in mind that goals can often be reached sequentially rather than simultaneously. In other words, what you don't chose at first, you might still be able to chose later: fix up your home now, buy the new computer next year.

It would be a great life if all our goal conflicts resulted from having desirable goals to choose from. However, in this not-so-perfect world, a second type of goal conflict is perhaps a bit more common: having to weigh the desirable part of a goal against the undesirable part. In this kind of conflict, you weigh possible gains against possible losses, and the potential for pleasure against the potential for pain. You weigh the "good" against the "bad," and you often find that you must "take the bitter with the sweet." A new computer might make it easier for you to bring work home from the office (desirable), and it sure would be nice to eliminate that leaky roof once and for all (desirable), but you're not excited about going into debt (undesirable) in order to purchase a new computer *and* fix up the house.

A third type of goal conflict arises when you are forced to choose between two goals that are both undesirable. You can probably remember some unpleasant time in your life when you remarked, "Huh, some choice!" Such a remark usually refers to a situation in which you're "damned if you do and damned if you don't." For example, a judge might ask, "Thirty days or $300." Or you may have to choose between living with a toothache or going to the dentist, or between having your truck repossessed or losing the station wagon. This third type of conflict usually creates the greatest amount of frustration and stress.

The ability to resolve these goal conflicts is closely related to your maturity level. If you are relatively immature, you will go to great lengths to avoid having to make the hard decisions. You will tend to procrastinate or even try to get someone else to make decisions for you. On the other hand, if you are relatively mature, you will usually accept responsibility for the decision and confront the unavoidable with necessary courage. If, for example, you have been laid off from work, you can wait until your creditors start pounding on your door, or you can call them immediately to let them know your situation. Taking the latter course allows you to explore their willingness to make adjustments in your payment schedules.

Putting It All Together

From early childhood, you were probably told that it's a cold, cruel world out there, and that physical, emotional, and economic survival is not easy. What you weren't told was just how hard it was going to be to put it all together.

Physical survival. Your ability to survive physically is determined by your ability to provide the necessities of life, such as food, clothing, and shelter; to provide medical and health care; and to prepare for retirement. To survive physically, then, you must provide the *means* to go on living.

Emotional survival. Your ability to survive emotionally is determined by your ability to provide a *reason* to go on living. Emotional survival depends on your ability to give meaning to life, establish satisfying relationships, and develop the courage to have faith in the future.

Economic survival. Economic survival depends on your ability to convert your mental and physical efforts into goals, services, and money so that you can take care of your physical and emotional needs within the framework of your values.

NOTES
1. Orthner, 1990; U.S. Department of Commerce, 1994.
2. Ashton, 1975.

WORKSHEET 1.1—VALUES INVENTORY

Read the following list of items. Decide which ten are most valuable to you. Rank these from 1 to 10 (1 being the most valuable) in the appropriate spaces in the *You* column. Next, decide which ten items are most valuable to your spouse. Rank these from 1 to 10 in the appropriate spaces in the *Your Spouse* column. Share your personal rankings with your spouse, then compare how you each thought the other responded.

YOU	YOUR SPOUSE	
____	____	A secure and comfortable retirement
____	____	A sense of equality in relationships
____	____	Emotional and sexual intimacy
____	____	A sense of accomplishment in life
____	____	A sense of independence and self-reliance
____	____	A meaningful love relationship
____	____	Financial security for the family
____	____	Happiness or contentedness
____	____	A meaningful relationship with God
____	____	Feelings of self-confidence
____	____	Social recognition and community status
____	____	A fulfilling marriage
____	____	Meaningful purpose in life
____	____	Helping the poor, sick, and disadvantaged
____	____	A sense of family togetherness and happy children
____	____	Learning, gaining knowledge continually
____	____	Honesty and personal integrity
____	____	Good health and physical fitness
____	____	Close relationships with extended family
____	____	Traveling and quality vacations
____	____	Companionship, spending time together as a couple
____	____	Success in a job or career
____	____	Freedom to live life as you choose
____	____	New experiences and adventures
____	____	Being outdoors, away from city life
____	____	Satisfying friendships, liking people, and being liked
____	____	Living in the city, access to restaurants and entertainment
____	____	Time alone, being by yourself
____	____	Having nice things, such as cars, boats, furniture
____	____	Emotional security, freedom from excessive stress

WORKSHEET 1.1—VALUES INVENTORY

Read the following list of items. Decide which ten are most valuable to you. Rank these from 1 to 10 (1 being the most valuable) in the appropriate spaces in the *You* column. Next, decide which ten items are most valuable to your spouse. Rank these from 1 to 10 in the appropriate spaces in the *Your Spouse* column. Share your personal rankings with your spouse, then compare how you each thought the other responded.

YOU	YOUR SPOUSE	
____	____	A secure and comfortable retirement
____	____	A sense of equality in relationships
____	____	Emotional and sexual intimacy
____	____	A sense of accomplishment in life
____	____	A sense of independence and self-reliance
____	____	A meaningful love relationship
____	____	Financial security for the family
____	____	Happiness or contentedness
____	____	A meaningful relationship with God
____	____	Feelings of self-confidence
____	____	Social recognition and community status
____	____	A fulfilling marriage
____	____	Meaningful purpose in life
____	____	Helping the poor, sick, and disadvantaged
____	____	A sense of family togetherness and happy children
____	____	Learning, gaining knowledge continually
____	____	Honesty and personal integrity
____	____	Good health and physical fitness
____	____	Close relationships with extended family
____	____	Traveling and quality vacations
____	____	Companionship, spending time together as a couple
____	____	Success in a job or career
____	____	Freedom to live life as you choose
____	____	New experiences and adventures
____	____	Being outdoors, away from city life
____	____	Satisfying friendships, liking people, and being liked
____	____	Living in the city, access to restaurants and entertainment
____	____	Time alone, being by yourself
____	____	Having nice things, such as cars, boats, furniture
____	____	Emotional security, freedom from excessive stress

CHAPTER 2

WHAT WE BRING WITH US

It does not take us long to realize that we do not enter marriage empty handed; we carry a lot of "baggage" with us. For instance, we bring our levels of self-esteem, our willingness to adapt to change, our attitudes toward life, and our expectations and values.

Unfortunately, many newlyweds tend to bring to their marriages a fairy-tale belief in living happily ever after, a belief seemingly based on this supposition: "We have been good. Therefore, only good things will happen to us." This belief seems to blind them to the fact that their relationship will undergo radical and usually unexpected changes. One partner may even naively ask the other to "stay just the way you are." (If this were to happen, the partner making the request would someday be married to a sixty-year-old spouse with the maturity of a twenty-year-old! Not a pretty picture.)

What usually prompts such a request is the desire to perpetuate the happiness the partner feels at that moment. Many erroneously assume that the state of being happy is *static* rather than *dynamic*, or changing. But life is change, and happiness is not fully appreciated in the absence of sorrow and hardship. Two people who go through life's ups and downs together grow in ways neither may foresee. Because each partner changes, they do not just celebrate an annual anniversary but rather what could be called a "remarriage."

Two people celebrating a fiftieth wedding anniversary, for example, are not the same two people who married at age eighteen. A pioneer woman who built sod huts, plowed fields, bore and buried children, fought off Indians, dug wells during droughts, and twice nursed her husband back to health would not be the same debutante her husband first met in a quaint St. Louis sitting room. Having been through such adversity together, however, they would most likely end up loving each other in a deeper, more personal way than when they first met. She would have changed, he would have changed, and their love would have changed. And with each change they would recommit—redeclare—their desire to be married to each other.

Family Rules

As you begin your transition from single life to married life with children, be assured you will have to overcome difficulties. Many of these difficulties may originate in something else you brought with you to your marriage: your separate sets of "family rules."

Because of your upbringing in your particular family (your "family of origin"), certain rules guide you in your social roles, govern your interpersonal relationships, set limits on your behavior, and enable you to reasonably predict the behavior of others. Among these family rules are expectations about how to manage your finances—and as you might have guessed, the rules each of you has "inherited" will most likely be different.

Often it is while making wedding plans that a couple first encounters differences in family rules. Some of these differences will create conflict *within* the individual, and some will create conflict *between* the individuals. Family rules are maintained and transmitted across generations on three levels: explicit, implicit, and intuitive.

Explicit Family Rules

Explicit family rules are expressed verbally or posted on the refrigerator door: "Don't talk with your mouth full. Don't whistle at the table. Sit up straight. Don't spend all your money on candy."

Explicit family rules concerning finances might include: "Save some of what you earn. Never buy on credit. Count your change before you leave the counter. Never lend money to a friend. Pay your debts on time. Don't buy things foolishly. And above all, don't talk to others about your personal financial affairs." (In this regard, Sigmund Freud said, "Money [matters] will be treated by cultured people in the same manner as sexual matters, with the same inconsistency, prudishness, and hypocrisy."[1]

Implicit Family Rules

Implicit family rules often have the greatest impact on our lives. Implicit rules are those taught through nonverbal communication and repeated throughout childhood. Implicit rules tend to be just below conscious awareness, so we seldom realize we are following them until someone points it out to us.

One example of an implicit rule is "When Dad leaves the room during an argument, that's the end of the discussion." Other implicit family rules might tell us that when Mom gets a tear in her eye, we do not pursue the issue any further. We also know which chair is Dad's. We know we should not compare Mom to her sister, bring up the name of a certain relative, or use certain tones of voice when talking to either parent. We know it is not permissible to stay out past midnight, kiss someone in public unless we are at an airport, or leave home permanently unless we're getting married, going to college, or joining the military.

Learning to manage finances begins at an early age. Some lessons are deliberately taught, but most financial management practices are implicitly passed—through example—from one generation to the next. Some men are "taught" in this way to turn their earnings over to their wife and let her run the house. Others are taught that the father manages the finances, and that the rest of the family lives off a specific allowance. Still others learn that marriage partners take care of their own income and expenses.

Implicit family rules about finances can be detected in such recollections as these: "Dad paid cash for everything. We never talked about money. We never knew how much money Dad made." "Mom never paid more than $20 for a pair of shoes. Mom paid the bills and kept the books. Dad turned his paycheck over to her." "We never went on expensive vacations. The family ate out only on special occasions." "All the relatives owned their own homes. We kept a car for at least five years." "Mom never bought anything for herself. The needs of the kids always came first."

Intuitive Family Rules

Like implicit rules, intuitive rules are also unspoken. But while implicit rules concern more everyday kinds of issues, intuitive rules concern those that are more far reaching. Based on family heritage—the *emotional legacy* inherited by each person—an implicit rule includes any "ledger" of instinctive obligations that needs to be balanced, any need to "pay back" something "owed" to another, or to "pass on" something of value or importance (such as traditions or beliefs). For example, some children feel an obligation to repay their parents for all the suffering and sacrifice on the children's behalf, or they feel a need to succeed in order to ensure that all the parents went through has not been in vain.

Our legacy may also include expectations associated with our ethnic, religious, or vocational backgrounds. How much should we contribute toward helping other members of the family come to America? Who will stay on the farm? Who is to become the next doctor? Our legacy can prompt additional questions: Who will take care of our parents or help pay off their debts? Who is going to see that the siblings get an education?

Intuitive rules also include family taboos: "Never marry someone of a different race (or religion, nationality, socioeconomic status)." "Never change your citizenship (or religion, politics, and so on)." "Never sell the land (or the house, a particular heirloom, or such)." "Never gamble and risk losing everything the way Grandpa did." "Even if you declare bankruptcy, your honor will demand that you repay those you owe."

Family Rules Inventory

To better understand how family rules influence your finances, you need to know what rules—explicit, implicit, and intuitive—you and your partner have brought to your marriage.

The following list of exploratory questions will help you identify family rules that govern specific topics and communication patterns. After considering these questions—and any additional ones you may think of—each of you should fill out a copy of Family Rules Inventory, Worksheet 2.1 (pages 43–44).

To make your answers as thorough as possible, talk to your brothers, sisters, and parents about your family's rules. (You may also find this worksheet helpful to list and discuss family rules in areas such as communication, sexuality, morality, health, or education. After you have completed the worksheet, compare and discuss your answers with your partner. Ask yourselves how you feel about these rules. Which ones do you want to keep for your new family, and which ones do you want to reject? Determine what compromises and accommodations you need to make.

Exploratory Questions

1. Do you think your family was materialistic? In what ways?

2. Could you ask for financial support? How did family members respond when another family member made a request for help?

3. How did you and your parents express affection for each other?

4. How did your parents express affection to each other?

5. Were you allowed to express your feelings? Which feelings and to whom?

6. How did your parents express approval or disapproval?

7. How did family members respond to change?

8. What kinds of roles were assigned to males and females?

9. How did your family evaluate success? In terms of money, degrees, land, social status, or possessions? In other ways?

10. How did your parents feel about debt?

11. How did your parents manage the family finances?

12. How openly could you talk about finances?

13. In which socioeconomic (middle class, upper class, etc.) group do you think your family belonged? During which period of your life?

14. What was your parents' attitude toward both husband and wife working outside the home?

15. What was your family's attitude toward saving and investing?

Rules as a Source of Conflict

Most families have hundreds of spoken and unspoken rules, and in many ways these rules help describe who we are. For instance, a woman raised in a small Japanese village would acquire social rules characteristically attributed to being Japanese. Similarly, a man raised in a small Swedish village would acquire rules that would make him Swedish. If both were to immigrate to the United States, they would take a great deal of their heritage with them and would need to adapt before they felt comfortable in their new communities.

A similar process often governs adaptation to a new marriage. In a way, each person's family of origin is like a "village" that supplies the rules brought to the marriage—rules that tend to bias perceptions and govern behavior. For example, when money got a little tight, Kent suggested that Keisha sell "that old hutch" so they could put the money to "good use." But Keisha cherished the hutch as an irreplaceable heirloom; she would never part with something her great-grandmother had hauled across the prairie in a covered wagon. "If you really loved me," she replied, "you would know how much that hutch means to me, and you would never even suggest selling it." Such statements can easily escalate into power struggles that end with such ultimatums as "I honestly think you love that hutch more than you love me. Well, it's either that thing or me. Make up your mind, because you can't have both."

In an attempt to cool things down, Keisha suggested that they borrow some money from their parents or friends. However, Kent had learned in childhood that you "never borrow money from friends or relatives," since this would inevitably destroy those relationships. Kent's belief in this rule placed powerful restraints on Keisha's suggestion. Keisha's failure to understand how important this rule was to Kent and Kent's insensitivity to Keisha's emotional bond with the hutch were a source of unending conflict. However, both were merely obeying family rules.

When Family Rules Are Broken

It is important that couples understand the rules that bias their perceptions, because these rules influence not only how they expect others to behave but also the consequences they mete out to those who break these rules. One of the most frequent consequences of breaking family rules is distancing by other family members. If, for example, someone were to wear Scandinavian logging boots into a Japanese house, the hosts might be offended and act somewhat cool and distant.

However, it is not necessary to wear logging boots into someone's house in order to end up being distanced; all you have to do is break family rules. For example, Maria invites her new boyfriend, Raphael, to dinner at her home for the first time. Raphael unknowingly sits in Maria's dad's chair, impudently calls him "Pops," and begins to eat before the others have been served or the food blessed. He has broken four family rules within thirty minutes. Some of the family members are not exactly sure why they have not taken to Raphael, but they all sense that he just doesn't fit in.

Jorge is introduced to the family a few weeks later. He remains standing until the mother has been seated, and he calls the father "sir." Jorge not only waits until after the food has been blessed before beginning to eat, but also compliments the cook and offers to help with the dishes after dinner. Everybody likes Jorge—he seems to be fit right in with the rest of the family.

The difference in the degree of acceptance afforded Raphael and Jorge reflects their irreverence toward or compliance with family rules. This is frequently true with regard to in-law relations, and it helps to explain why some sons- or daughters-in-law are accepted into a family and others are not. The degree of harmony between the husband's family rules and the wife's family rules also greatly determines the degree of difficulty in adjusting to marriage. Consider the following examples:

1. The husband and wife are operating under the rules they brought with them from their families of origin. They do not try to understand or acknowledge each other's rules.

Paul greets Helen coolly. "You're home late."

Helen stretches and tries to ignore his coolness. "I know. I had a lot to do today."

"You're supposed to call when you're going to be late."

Unwilling to ignore the implied accusation, Helen counters, "What are you getting so upset about? I thought you said you were going to support me in this new job. Coming home to harassment is not what I call support!"

Paul's family rule: Spouses call when they will be home late.

Helen's family rule: Spouses support each other's efforts without placing limits.

2. The husband and wife are also operating under separate family rules, but they try to check out their assumptions about how the other should behave.

Wiping her hands on her apron, Fatima greets Ali at the kitchen doorway. "You're home late."

Ali says tiredly, "I know. I had a lot to do today."

"I know you're busy," Fatima says carefully, "but I'm still upset that you didn't call. Did you know that I'd like you to call when you'll be late?"

"No, I didn't realize that. My dad always just came home as soon as he could, and my mom was always flexible with dinner."

Fatima hesitates for a moment, then presents her position. "I'm willing to be flexible with dinner, but I would also like to know when I can expect you to be home. Would you be willing to call me the next time you'll be home later than 6:30?"

"Sure. I'm sorry I didn't think to call tonight."

Fatima smiles her appreciation. "Thanks. It would make it a lot easier for me to make plans for the evening."

Fatima's family rule: Spouses call when they are going to be late.

Ali's family rule: Spouses do the best they can and need to be flexible with their expectations.

Rule for the new family of Fatima and Ali: Consideration of each other's needs and feelings is more important than loyalty to the way their parents did things.

Coping with Family Financial Rules

It is imperative that you come to know your spouse's family financial rules. In most cases, when a spouse breaks the other's rules, it is out of ignorance and quite unintentional. Nevertheless, it can lead to a state of perpetual discord. Having a knowledge of your spouse's rules can enable you to express love and consideration in ways that can be more fully understood and appreciated by both of you.

The following list of suggestions can help you and your partner make conscious choices about the financial rules and management patterns that will characterize your marriage.

Financial Management Suggestions

1. Be aware that each of us has an assortment of divergent values, standards, and goals that tend to influence the way we want resources allocated.

2. Accept that each of us comes to marriage with a unique set of financial rules.

3. Appreciate the severe stress placed on individuals and families when family financial rules are broken.

4. Understand that it is possible for families and family members to modify their financial management procedures.

5. Assess the financial management patterns of your family of origin, and determine which of these you wish to perpetuate or discard.

6. Develop a family plan designed to alter existing, dysfunctional financial patterns and establish functional financial management techniques.

7. Learn as a family how to effectively plan, control, and evaluate the management of financial resources.

Birth Order and Financial Issues

Family rules aren't the only things we bring to our marriages from our families of origin. We also bring the characteristics we acquire through our birth-order position in the family. Personality characteristics associated with our birth order can have a profound influence on how we manage our finances. These characteristics, developed in childhood, are often a permanent part of our adult life.

Birth-Order Clusters

The important role that birth order plays in our lives has been explored by a number of psychologists. They have determined that birth order can have a major influence on the development of certain personality characteristics.[2] These personality characteristics can have a profound influence on how financial resources are managed. The most easily identifiable birth-order positions are the *firstborn, second born, middle born,* and *last born.*

The Firstborn. Firstborn children are often asked to take care of younger siblings, so being in control and taking charge comes easily to them. Managing the checkbook, giving out allowances, paying the bills, developing a budget (and making sure everyone adheres to its guidelines) and other financial management tasks come naturally to the eldest child. Firstborn children tend to be ambitious and high achievers. Research indicates that firstborn individuals attain higher rates of salary increase than individuals of other birth orders.[3]

Many firstborns tend to go overboard with their need to control, wanting to be in charge of everything and everyone, including themselves. In fact, firstborn children who develop an exaggerated need to control will often take great pride in what they refer to as self-control—the ability to withstand the urge to purchase wants or luxuries. To these individuals, self-control means sticking with the basics and purchasing only things they truly need. They consider impulse buying an absolute no-no, and they consider those who so indulge as weak and worthy of criticism. Those who exercise this type of control to the extreme live a miserly existence characterized by exaggerated savings programs and austere surroundings. They may decide to keep an older car, for example, spending more to maintain it than they would to buy a new car.

Firstborns with a need for control often face the dilemma of being overwhelmed with managing finances, yet are afraid of losing control if some of the responsibilities are allocated to others. Some control-oriented people believe that the one who controls the purse strings controls all. They want to make others subservient, often through control of the checkbook, credit cards, allowances, or distribution of inheritance. While they may keep income confidential, they make expenses public in a gloomy, pessimistic light. For example, no one in the family knows for sure just how much money Dad makes, yet whenever family members ask to buy something they are told, "I can barely pay the monthly bills let alone have enough left over to spend on luxuries."

Unfortunately, living under the influence of a control-oriented individual often creates tension and feelings of frustration. Tired of being stifled by rigid financial programs, family members may become defiant and rebellious, go on spending sprees, or juggle the books.

If you think you have an exaggerated need for control and are encountering defiance in others, it is time to develop a more cooperative, democratic approach toward finances and relationships. You may wish to start by (1) bringing financial matters into open discussion, (2) developing a financial management plan based on distributing financial responsibilities among all family members, and (3) giving each family member some kind of allowance to spend as they wish.

The technique of "trading places," or rotating leadership roles, can also be useful in achieving a more egalitarian atmosphere while managing finances. Controllers have a strong desire to avoid ridicule or humiliation, so they must learn to accept their human weaknesses. A control-oriented person needs to develop the courage to be imperfect, to make mistakes and still remain lovable. Everyone needs to agree that the world will not end if one of you makes a decision that ends up costing the family more than was expected. No one is immune to buyer's remorse.

The Second Born. Second-born children hate being controlled or having someone tell them what to do. Because they are quite independent, they want to spend money without having to account for it. They have been known to sabotage many firstborn's plans to keep things—including budgets—organized. Second borns can spend a lot of money trying to look as good as someone else.

Many second-born children develop the belief that being number one is everything. They want to be the best and have the best in order to feel good about themselves. This belief system can prove expensive. Such individuals often find themselves compelled to purchase top-of-the-line items even when they cannot afford them. They acquire quality not just for quality's sake but rather to gain recognition and esteem associated with prestigious items. Brand names and labels, and the location of stores are important to them.

Second-born individuals with this orientation do not want to merely keep up with the Joneses, they want to surpass them. They often find themselves participating in an undeclared, progressively expensive, game of one-upmanship. At the beginning of the game, they may ask themselves, "How do I measure up? Am I as good as others?" In answer, they engage in compulsive purchasing. If a sibling buys a new pickup, this kind of individual has to buy an even better pickup.

Some say that those who play this game are trying to compensate for feelings of inferiority. Yet by playing, they set themselves up to fail and to make comparisons in which eventually they will lose. For example, people who think this way and own a Cadillac will compare themselves with people who drive Ferraris or Rolls Royces—automobiles they cannot afford—rather than with owners of Volkswagens or Chevrolets. Unfortunately, even when they cannot afford a purchase, they will often make it anyway, setting up a pattern of spending beyond their means. They may send their children to the best schools, or become members of a particular country club, even though initiation fees or dues exceed what they can manage with their current income. As you might expect, this kind of behavior leads to chronic indebtedness, harassment from creditors, feelings of apprehension, and increased levels of marital stress.

If you recognize this personality characteristic in yourself and wish to overcome it, you must first become aware of how it affects spending behavior. You may find it helpful to review the social motivations behind particular purchases or buying habits, then compare these motivations with more practical reasons for making purchases. For example, what is your motive for buying a car? Is it to impress neighbors and relatives and to drive up to the country club in something that looks like it belongs there? Or is your motive to have a dependable means of transportation? From a practical standpoint, a five-year-old Chevrolet will get you across town about as well as a new BMW. The social reasons for wanting a BMW may originate in the need to feel superior.

Once you have greater insight into your motivations, you may realize you have a choice. You can continue behaving as you have in the past, which means continuing a life of futile comparisons, heavy debt, and stress. Or you can begin identifying how much status would—or should—honestly be enough for you (see chapter 6). Keep in mind Principle 6: You can never get enough of what you don't need, because what you don't need can never satisfy you.

The Middle Born. Middle-born children tend to go along with whatever budget has been established. They may resent the fact that their needs have been lost in the "needs of the family," but that is a familiar situation for middle-born children. However, because they are so sensitive to injustice and unfairness, they are more likely to stand up for the financial rights of other family members.

Some middle-born individuals may distort their willingness to be peacemakers—and to go along with the desires of others—into a dysfunctional desire to please others. Wanting to be accepted and liked by others becomes a top priority. They end up doing just about anything in order to avoid being rejected, often believing that they can buy the love and acceptance of others with gifts. Such individuals unfortunately see love as a commodity that can be bought, sold, and exchanged for goods and services, and their attempts to buy love can lead to financial disaster. Unfortunately, middle-born individuals unable to afford their own generosity find themselves on a treadmill, managing to pay off last Christmas at about the time the next Christmas rolls around.

If such individuals are parents, they usually accumulate heavy debt trying to satisfy the family's wishes, believing that children will interpret "No" as a lack of love. They may buy gifts for their spouses even if doing so requires working extra hours.

The "generosity" of these individuals can extend well beyond their immediate family. Pleasing-oriented people often lend money to neighbors, even if their own families are in great financial need. The situation worsens if the individuals making loans become reluctant to ask for repayment for fear of offending the debtors. Problems also arise when these individuals co-sign for loans, put up collateral for other people's loans, or take out loans in order to provide money for others.

In their efforts to avoid rejection, they may buy things they don't want or need simply because they want the salesperson to like them. This tendency makes them susceptible to high-pressure sales promotions and get-rich-quick schemes. As long as they believe they have to buy affection, they will find it difficult to distinguish between being valued for their personality and their possessions. Do their "friends" come over to be with them or to swim in their pool? Do their neighbors enjoy their company or their ski boat? Are their children as glad to see them come home empty-handed as they are when they come bearing gifts?

If you have pleasing tendencies and want to confront them, you may wish to find out if a failure to "come through" with a gift or loan would end a particular relationship. If so, you may ask yourself, "What is the merit in maintaining such a relationship?" Rather than being afraid of rejection, you may find it helpful to actually seek rejection. See how many "friends" you can lose in a week merely by requesting payment from people who owe you money, or by saying no to requests for financial aid.

You must realize that a need to be liked by everyone (including those you dislike) indicates low self-esteem. Only by presenting yourself without gifts will you ever know the true basis of your relationships. Whether another person is happy, sad, loving, or rejecting is a choice that person makes; it is not within your power to generate those feelings. When you recognize that you cannot buy love and friendship, and that you cannot make someone else happy, you become more able to question the motivation behind your gift exchanges and loans. With enough encouragement and change in outlook, your primary concern can become the welfare of others rather than whether you are accepted or rejected.

The Last Born. The last-born child is often used to being pampered and treated like a prince or princess. It is not unusual for youngest children to "max out" their credit limits—and then some. One study found that last-born children have higher average total liabilities and a higher debt-to-income ratio than individuals in any other birth-order position.[4]

Because many youngest children are pampered, they tend to be self-indulgent and fail to discriminate between needs and wants. Such individuals often have a history of impulsive buying; the very desire for something is sufficient reason to purchase it. People buy impulsively partly to acquire the desired item as soon as possible, and partly to reduce the stress from not having what they want.

Last-born individuals tend to live for today and often believe that there really is such a thing as a free lunch and that the piper doesn't necessarily have to be paid. The day of reckoning, however, eventually arrives. As a consequence, stress reduction is one of the primary goals of pampered youngest children. But they often procrastinate, hoping that whatever is causing stress will go away if they ignore it. As a consequence, they often accumulate unfinished business, unresolved problems, and unmade decisions. Thinking to ease their stress as quickly as possible and at any cost, they refinance loans, take out additional loans, or consolidate existing loans. They ask for cash advances on salaries, delay payments on bills, and pawn valued possessions. They do not open mail or answer the phone, and they can get quite good at lying.

Pampered youngest look for the so-called "easy" way out. They may walk out on current debts, move to another state, and start over. They often view bankruptcy as a way to escape the stress of heavy indebtedness rather than as a way to solve current financial problems and get a fresh start. Usually they see their negative financial situation as only temporary; they believe their ship will come in "any day now."

To counter these tendencies, if you have them, recognize that one of the most efficient ways to reduce stress is to act responsibly. Ask yourself, "How would things be different if I were to have all of my debts paid off and I were no longer being harassed by creditors?" or "How would my life be different if I were able to increase my income by 20 percent or reduce my spending by 10 percent?"

Remember, however, that if you are a youngest child, you may tend to resist structured or limiting corrective programs. Any remedial programs you adopt should not be too austere. You may find that, for you, increasing income may be more effective than reducing expenditures.

Table 2.1—BIRTH ORDER AND FINANCIAL ISSUES

BIRTH ORDER	CONTROL ISSUES	BUDGETING	NEEDS/WANTS
Firstborn	Is in control, takes charge, manages the checkbook, pays the bills.	Makes out a budget, makes sure everyone adheres to it.	Conservative; takes care of needs first, saves before buying.
Second Born	Hates being controlled, likes to have personal money.	Sometimes sabotages the firstborn's budget.	Impatient, experiences severe stress if unable to satisfy wants.
Middle Born	Assumes responsibility for management tasks.	Tends to go along with whatever budget is established.	Sensitive to fairness, considers equally everyone's needs.
Last Born	Doesn't like controls, prefers to operate on impulse.	Sees budgets as restrictive; avoids responsibility.	Does not distinguish between needs and wants.

Interaction Patterns

It's not too hard to imagine what kind of interaction might occur when an individual with one set of birth-order characteristics marries someone with a different set. Preliminary research shows that birth order can affect family finances. For instance, a couple's birth-order combination is a significant predictor of family income. Last-born husbands married to middle-born wives have the highest family incomes, while middle-born husbands with firstborn wives have the lowest.[5]

Similarly, a firstborn who marries another firstborn may end up in a marriage that has two generals fighting for control. A firstborn who marries a second born may end up looking like the odd couple. A firstborn who marries a last born may develop a parent-child type of relationship. A last born who marries another last born may fall into a lifestyle of overindulgence and debt.

An example of the parent-child dilemma can be illustrated with Adam and Tashi's relationship. Adam and Tashi were on the verge of divorce because of what Tashi saw as Adam's irresponsible use of the checking account. "No one in my family *ever* bounced a check," Tashi growled. "I've never in my life been so embarrassed as when the Salvation Army returned our donation check due to *insufficient funds*." Tashi was a firstborn child who acted responsibly, and she expected others to behave in an equally responsible manner.

Adam, on the other hand, was the youngest child in his family of origin. He had a difficult time understanding why Tashi could get so angry with him over a "little" thing like bouncing a check. He countered her accusations with his own indignation. "Lots of people bounce checks. No big deal. It's a perfectly natural, human mistake."

The Birth-Order Exercise

The Birth-Order Exercise, Worksheets 2.2 through 2.5 (pages 45–48), will help you identify the characteristics you developed in your family of origin, and will help you apply this knowledge to your marital and financial relationships. The Birth-Order Exercise has four versions—one for each birth-order cluster. Fill out the version that pertains to your birth order. Then fill out one for your spouse, indicating which characteristics for his or her birth order match his or her personality.

Financially Effective Personality Characteristics

My neighbor, a certified public accountant, once said that from a financial standpoint there are really only two kinds of people: *spenders* and *savers*. He maintains that spenders tend to be in debt, live from paycheck to paycheck, and have little or nothing available for investment. Savers, however, tend to pay cash for what they buy, maintain a savings account, and remain financially secure thanks to long-term investments.

Being a saver is one favorable trait, but a variety of personality characteristics can contribute to effective financial management behaviors. These characteristics include:

Self-reliance. If you are self-reliant, you try to be your own banker whenever possible, establishing a savings program and setting aside "payments" toward the purchase of an item long before you actually buy it. In this way, you can earn interest rather than pay it.

Accurate perception of reality. It's important to appreciate the need to live on your *net income* (what's left of your paycheck after taxes, Social Security, pension payments, and dues are taken out). It's also important that you be able to accurately appraise the *true* cost of a purchase (including taxes, interest, operation, insurance premiums, and accessories; see chapter 6), and recognize and adapt to any change in your financial situation.

Flexibility. If you live below your means, you are able to draw on uncommitted funds as the need arises. You are then able to enjoy the freedom and flexibility that come from a lack of indebtedness. As you grow and change, your plans and goals are able to grow and change with you.

Problem-centeredness. Problem-centered people can distinguish between the things they can do something about and the things they can do nothing about. For example, you cannot do much about factory shutdowns or layoffs, but you can do a great deal to establish a family emergency fund for use in such a situation.

Active appreciation. Active appreciation means that you consistently value what you own. You remember that "new and improved" models are not necessarily preferable to what you already have. You appreciate utilitarian value as well as aesthetic value. You recognize the importance of taking care of your possessions and maintaining them properly to prolong their life expectancy and keep replacement costs at a minimum.

Strong sense of ethics. You know how important it is to be honest in all your financial dealings. You believe that no financial gain is worth sacrificing valued relationships, self-respect, or personal integrity.

Strong sense of self. By maintaining your individuality and a strong sense of self, you can suppress the urge to waste money on fads, status symbols, or competition with others.

Imagination. By being imaginative and creative in increasing your income or decreasing your spending, you can better cope with changes in the economic climate. You are willing to try a variety of things, from being artistic to taking classes in home and car maintenance, from holding garage sales to making needed items at home.

Appreciation of emotional costs. It is essential that you develop the ability to evaluate the emotional costs as well as the monetary costs of an item. Consider the emotional strain placed on a family because of increased indebtedness or additional work hours. Consider what others may have to give up because of someone else's spending habits.

Charity. You have a sense of belonging to humanity. Giving to charitable causes is part of your resolution to serve the needs of others. You recognize that your own well-being is intimately involved with that of others—especially family members. You find little comfort in overeating while watching others starve.

The Task Satisfaction Scale

Frequently, people assume responsibility for certain tasks based on their birth order or on observation of their parents. However, they may not necessarily like the tasks they have assumed.

The Managerial Task Satisfaction Scale, Worksheet 2.6 (pages 49–50), will help you pinpoint how you feel about the allocation of financial management tasks in your family and how you believe your spouse feels about assigned tasks. You should each complete a copy of the worksheet. Then compare and discuss your responses. If one of you is particularly averse to a certain task, such as balancing the checkbook or paying bills, being asked to perform this task may create feelings of resentment and distance. You might either share the task or allocate it to the other partner. With more open communication, you can avoid such problems.

NOTES

1. Freud, 1913, 283.
2. Adler, 1927.
3. Berger and Ivancevich, 1973.
4. Poduska and Allred, 1987.
5. Steggell, Allred, Harper, and Poduska, 1990.

WORKSHEET 2.1—FAMILY RULES INVENTORY

List as many financial rules from your family of origin as you can recall in each of the three categories. If you need more space, use the back of the worksheet or other sheets of paper.

EXPLICIT FAMILY RULES

1. _____
2. _____
3. _____
4. _____
5. _____
6. _____
7. _____
8. _____
9. _____
10. _____

IMPLICIT FAMILY RULES

1. _____
2. _____
3. _____
4. _____
5. _____
6. _____
7. _____
8. _____
9. _____
10. _____

INTUITIVE FAMILY RULES

1. _____
2. _____
3. _____
4. _____
5. _____
6. _____
7. _____
8. _____
9. _____
10. _____

WORKSHEET 2.1—FAMILY RULES INVENTORY

List as many financial rules from your family of origin as you can recall in each of the three categories. If you need more space, use the back of the worksheet or other sheets of paper.

EXPLICIT FAMILY RULES

1. _____
2. _____
3. _____
4. _____
5. _____
6. _____
7. _____
8. _____
9. _____
10. _____

IMPLICIT FAMILY RULES

1. _____
2. _____
3. _____
4. _____
5. _____
6. _____
7. _____
8. _____
9. _____
10. _____

INTUITIVE FAMILY RULES

1. _____
2. _____
3. _____
4. _____
5. _____
6. _____
7. _____
8. _____
9. _____
10. _____

WORKSHEET 2.2—BIRTH ORDER EXERCISE (FIRSTBORN)

This sheet lists characteristics common in firstborn children. If you are completing this exercise for yourself, read each description and decide how characteristic it is of you. If it is not at all characteristic, circle 1 on the scale. If it describes you exactly, circle 5. If you are somewhere in between, circle 2, 3, or 4. If you are completing this exercise for your partner, indicate instead how characteristic the description is of him or her.

HOW CHARACTERISTIC IS THIS OF ME/MY PARTNER?

	NOT AT ALL				EXACTLY
A firstborn person:					
1. Needs to be "in charge" or "the boss."	1	2	3	4	5
2. Feels threatened by criticism from others.	1	2	3	4	5
3. Is cautious, does not like to take risks.	1	2	3	4	5
4. Tries to get as much information as possible in order to make plans and lists.	1	2	3	4	5
5. Tends to be intellectual; likes to work with facts and data.	1	2	3	4	5
6. Feels responsible for making sure everything turns out well; fearful of being wrong or making mistakes.	1	2	3	4	5
7. Is obedient, oriented to rules and authority.	1	2	3	4	5
8. Is conservative; does not like things to change or happen unexpectedly.	1	2	3	4	5
9. Is ambitious and a high achiever.	1	2	3	4	5
10. Has a tendency to feel superior to others.	1	2	3	4	5

WORKSHEET 2.3—BIRTH ORDER EXERCISE (SECOND BORN)

This sheets lists characteristics common in second-born children. If you are completing this exercise for yourself, read each description and decide how characteristic it is of you. If it is not at all characteristic, circle 1 on the scale. If it describes you exactly, circle 5. If you are somewhere in between, circle 2, 3, or 4. If you are completing this exercise for your partner, indicate instead how characteristic the description is of him or her.

HOW CHARACTERISTIC IS THIS OF ME/MY PARTNER?

	NOT AT ALL				EXACTLY
A second-born person:					
1. Is the opposite of his or her older sibling.	1	2	3	4	5
2. Is rebellious, liberal thinking, and willing to try something new.	1	2	3	4	5
3. Is stubborn.	1	2	3	4	5
4. Is very competitive.	1	2	3	4	5
5. Is assertive and outspoken.	1	2	3	4	5
6. Gets bored easily.	1	2	3	4	5
7. Has his or her individual interpretation of the rules.	1	2	3	4	5
8. Is impulsive and often does not think of the consequences.	1	2	3	4	5
9. Needs to be given choices rather than be told what to do.	1	2	3	4	5
10. Sees situations in terms of black and white; there is no middle ground.	1	2	3	4	5

WORKSHEET 2.4—BIRTH ORDER EXERCISE (MIDDLE BORN)

This sheet lists characteristics common in middle-born children. If you are completing this exercise for yourself, read each description and decide how characteristic it is of you. If it is not at all characteristic, circle 1 on the scale. If it describes you exactly, circle 5. If you are somewhere in between, circle 2, 3, or 4. If you are completing this exercise for your partner, indicate instead how characteristic the description is of him or her.

How characteristic is this of me/my partner?

	Not at All				Exactly
A middle-born person:					
1. Is easygoing and does not get upset over the "little things."	1	2	3	4	5
2. Is willing to negotiate and compromise.	1	2	3	4	5
3. Needs to feel appreciated.	1	2	3	4	5
4. Likes to be different.	1	2	3	4	5
5. Is independent.	1	2	3	4	5
6. Tends to be accepting of self and others.	1	2	3	4	5
7. Has an identity problem; often feels "invisible."	1	2	3	4	5
8. Will urge a compromise and rarely takes a stand in the family.	1	2	3	4	5
9. Sees life as a struggle.	1	2	3	4	5
10. Tends to take a holistic view of things.	1	2	3	4	5

WORKSHEET 2.5—BIRTH ORDER EXERCISE (LAST BORN)

This sheet lists characteristics common in youngest children. If you are completing this exercise for yourself, read each description and decide how characteristic it is of you. If it is not at all characteristic, circle 1 on the scale. If it describes you exactly, circle 5. If you are somewhere in between, circle 2, 3, or 4. If you are completing this exercise for your partner, indicate instead how characteristic the description is of him or her.

HOW CHARACTERISTIC IS THIS OF ME/MY PARTNER?

	NOT AT ALL				EXACTLY
A youngest, or last-born, person:					
1. Is charming and likeable.	1	2	3	4	5
2. Is impatient; wants something now.	1	2	3	4	5
3. Is very imaginative, creative, and inventive.	1	2	3	4	5
4. Is self-indulgent; believes that he or she is special.	1	2	3	4	5
5. Is irresponsible and undependable; does not believe that he or she should have to pay the consequences for behavior.	1	2	3	4	5
6. Is courageous, not afraid of failure.	1	2	3	4	5
7. Has often been spoiled and pampered.	1	2	3	4	5
8. Does not believe that he or she is taken seriously.	1	2	3	4	5
9. Feels a need to outdo others.	1	2	3	4	5
10. Is manipulative; tries to get his or her own way.	1	2	3	4	5

WORKSHEET 2.6—MANAGERIAL TASK SATISFACTION SCALE

Who performs each of the following management tasks in your home? Are you satisfied with the way responsibilities are shared or divided? On a scale of 1 to 5, with 1 being "completely unhappy" and 5 being "completely happy," rate your satisfaction with each situation by circling the appropriate number. Then rate how you believe your spouse would respond by placing an *X* on the appropriate number.

	COMPLETELY UNHAPPY			COMPLETELY HAPPY	
1 Shopping for, buying groceries.	1	2	3	4	5
2. Obtaining maintenance, service, and repairs for the car(s)	1	2	3	4	5
3. Shopping for, selecting, and purchasing new or used cars.	1	2	3	4	5
4. Studying, deciding on, and investing in property, stocks, and bonds.	1	2	3	4	5
5. Studying, deciding on, and purchasing life, hospital, and medical insurance.	1	2	3	4	5
6. Studying, deciding on, and purchasing car, fire, liability, and other property insurance.	1	2	3	4	5
7. Figuring annual federal and state income taxes.	1	2	3	4	5
8. Maintaining records of income and expenses.	1	2	3	4	5
9. Preparing monthly or annual budget.	1	2	3	4	5
10. Paying bills.	1	2	3	4	5
11. Writing checks and making deposits.	1	2	3	4	5
12. Earning money through employment.	1	2	3	4	5
13. Assuming responsibility for family estate, will, and related matters.	1	2	3	4	5
14. Obtaining medical and dental care.	1	2	3	4	5
15. Managing family time commitments.	1	2	3	4	5
16. Deciding on and performing *inside* chores.	1	2	3	4	5
17. Deciding on and performing *outside* chores.	1	2	3	4	5

WORKSHEET 2.6—MANAGERIAL TASK SATISFACTION SCALE

Who performs each of the following management tasks in your home? Are you satisfied with the way responsibilities are shared or divided? On a scale of 1 to 5, with 1 being "completely unhappy" and 5 being "completely happy," rate your satisfaction with each situation by circling the appropriate number. Then rate how you believe your spouse would respond by placing an *X* on the appropriate number.

	COMPLETELY UNHAPPY				COMPLETELY HAPPY
1. Shopping for, buying groceries.	1	2	3	4	5
2. Obtaining maintenance, service, and repairs for the car(s).	1	2	3	4	5
3. Shopping for, selecting, and purchasing new or used cars.	1	2	3	4	5
4. Studying, deciding on, and investing in property, stocks, and bonds.	1	2	3	4	5
5. Studying, deciding on, and purchasing life, hospital, and medical insurance.	1	2	3	4	5
6. Studying, deciding on, and purchasing car, fire, liability, and other property insurance.	1	2	3	4	5
7. Figuring annual federal and state income taxes.	1	2	3	4	5
8. Maintaining records of income and expenses.	1	2	3	4	5
9. Preparing monthly or annual budget.	1	2	3	4	5
10. Paying bills.	1	2	3	4	5
11. Writing checks and making deposits	1	2	3	4	5
12. Earning money through employment.	1	2	3	4	5
13. Assuming responsibility for family estate, will, and related matters.	1	2	3	4	5
14. Obtaining medical and dental care.	1	2	3	4	5
15. Managing family time commitments.	1	2	3	4	5
16. Deciding on and performing *inside* chores.	1	2	3	4	5
17. Deciding on and performing *outside* chores.	1	2	3	4	5

CHAPTER 3

FAMILY RELATIONSHIPS AND FINANCES

Chapter 1 pointed out that many surveys find finances to be one of the major causes of marital discord and dissatisfaction—and even the leading cause of divorce. Why is this so? The answer often centers on the financial issues of *allocation* and *control*, which have roots in our personal relationships.

Allocation and Control

The process of allocating funds is linked to the principle of scarcity: the more resources you commit to A, the fewer you have to commit to B; the more you spend on new clothes, the less you have to spend on food. When faced with decisions related to this principle, you weigh the cost of giving up one option against the cost of giving up another. This is commonly referred to as *opportunity costs.*

Along with distinguishing between wants and needs (see chapter 8), you need to consider opportunity costs when establishing allocation (spending) priorities, such as what gets purchased first, who gets paid first (or at all), and whose values get satisfied first. But in the very act of trying to establish such priorities, concerns about control will arise almost automatically.

Allocation

For the most part, allocation issues are a middle-class phenomenon. Most of the time the poor have only enough to provide for their basic needs (food, clothing, and shelter); setting priorities for wants is usually not an issue, simply because there is nothing left to spend. The rich, on the other hand, usually have enough to take care of their needs and to satisfy their wants as well; they also do not have much need to set priorities. For the middle-class people, however, allocation is a problem, because although they may have enough for their basic needs, they seldom have enough left over to satisfy everyone's wants. They must somehow decide how to allocate remaining resources.

Control

Control deals with the problem of deciding not only who will establish priorities but who will actually oversee the allocation of funds. The possibility always exists that whoever has control may try to satisfy his or her own values before considering the values of others. To effectively cope with this inherent problem, we must look at the issue of dominance and submission.

Dominance and Submission

Cooperation, understanding, and consideration are essential to solving allocation problems. Partners cooperate most effectively when they consider themselves equals, and when both are capable of assuming dominant or submissive roles, depending on circumstances. Dominant and submissive roles should not be seen as positions of superiority and inferiority but as *reciprocal roles of responsibility*, as described in these guidelines:

1. Dominance does *not* mean being superior or a dictator.

2. Dominance means *consenting* to assume responsible leadership regarding the welfare of others.

3. Submission does *not* mean being inferior or a slave.

4. Submission means *consenting* to follow as long as your feelings and needs are considered.

Only in relationships based on equality can trust and intimacy exist. A dominant position in this kind of relationship, therefore, is not a tyrannical one, and submissiveness is not slavery. Self-appointed dictators are primarily concerned with their own welfare; those who *consent* to accept a dominant position—by a mutual decision of those involved in the relationship—are consenting to assume responsibility for the welfare of others. Similarly, individuals who consent to submission in a relationship are *not* abdicating their right to self-determination. On the contrary, they have consented to be submissive because they believe their feelings and needs will be considered. When individuals suspect that this is not the case, they usually withdraw their consent.

The person who has consented to be submissive may find it helpful to ask the following questions of the person who has consented to be dominant:

1. Have you made a decision?
2. Were my feelings considered?
3. Was the decision made with love (and not power)?

If the answer to all three questions is yes, the one in the submissive role can often sustain the decision even before finding out what was decided. The submissive party believes the dominant person has made the best decision possible, and does not indulge in recriminations if the decision results in problems. We may not always know what is the best decision or the worst. We may never know, for instance, what might have happened had we chosen differently. We only know what has happened as a result of the alternative we chose. So it is only in retrospect, after we see the consequences of a decision, that we can accurately evaluate our choices.

Consenting to be submissive or dominant obviously requires a great deal of trust, the courage to be vulnerable, a willingness to exchange the roles of leader and follower, and a commitment to establishing a relationship based on love rather than on power.

Love versus Power

If you trust the love in your relationship, you trust that the other person will not only try to satisfy your needs but will also *want* you to have what would make you happy. Even when you have no way of obtaining what you seek, the person who loves you will still *want* you to have it.

If, however, you do not trust the love in your relationship, you feel you must rely on yourself to satisfy your needs. You rely more on power than on love. If the other person won't give you what you want, then you feel that you have to either get it yourself or manipulate the other person into getting it for you. In either case, you may succeed in getting what you want, but you can never succeed in making the other person *want* you to have it. Only when we love someone does that person's happiness become as important as our own.

Imagine trying to sustain a marriage based solely on power. One partner might say: "I'll be the only one to write checks," "I'll decide how the money will be spent," or "I'll determine whether to tell you how much I earn." Imagine the following saying—handed down from generation to generation—done in needlepoint and hung on your wall: *I want you to have power over others as I have had power over you.*

Now imagine a relationship based on love. Discussions would include such questions as "How would you feel about my buying a new set of reference books?" or "Now that we have come into a little extra money, how would you like to see some of it spent?" Imagine the needlepoint saying *I want you to love others, as I have loved you.* When the feelings of all family members are considered in decision making, the family can experience solidarity and cohesiveness.

Moral Reasoning and Relationships

The need to be loved is the need for understanding from someone who cares. To be loved is to know that someone else is interested in your problems and frustrations as well as in your dreams and ambitions, to have another person show concern for your welfare and appreciation for your efforts.

If a relationship lacks reciprocation or consideration, however, concern can become indifference, appreciation can become contempt, and caring can turn into feelings of bitter sacrifice. These unfortunate transitions are usually the result of selfishness and a lack of moral maturity. The relative success or failure of a couple's relationship depends greatly on the degree of maturity each partner possesses.

Child development specialist Lawrence Kohlberg saw moral maturity as the ability to accurately perceive the appropriateness of one's action or inaction,[1] an ability developed from social maturation and the growth of *moral reasoning.* Kohlberg believed that an individual's moral reasoning progresses through six stages. We can use these stages of moral reasoning to evaluate interpersonal relationships.

Stage 1: Avoiding Punishment

At the lowest stage, Stage 1, moral reasoning is based on personal fear and the desire to avoid punishment. If your relationship operates at this level, you act morally only if you think you would be caught acting otherwise. For instance, you may be faithful to your spouse while in your hometown, but when you are out of town you may think that anything goes. Or you may reveal to your spouse all income from your regular job, but if you were to make a little money on the side (which is less easily detected), you would keep it secret.

Stage 2: Self-gratification

Stage 2's moral reasoning also has an *egocentric*, or self-centered, motive: "What's in it for me?" Operating at this level, you are nice to someone only if it will benefit you. You give to someone only if you think you will get something of equal or greater value in return. For instance, you are nice to your boss, to rich friends, and to those with influence because of their potential to reward you. But you see no purpose in being nice to those who work under you, to "friends" who are temporarily down on their luck, or to those with little or no influence.

The husband of a young couple provides a good example of a relationship based on self-gratification. Linda and Bill are living in student housing and are one month behind on their rent. Linda is working to put her husband through college, so money is scarce and "making do" has become routine. When she comes home from work, Bill meets her at the front door. Stopping her before she can get through the doorway, he excitedly tells her, "Don't come in yet! I've got a surprise for you." Bill then asks her to shut her eyes and, taking her by the hand, leads her into the living room. "Stand still and keep your eyes shut," he says. A moment later Linda is blasted with 100 watts of compact disc high fidelity generated by state-of-the-art matching tweeters and two 18-inch woofers. The stereo was something Bill had really wanted, and besides, it was on sale.

A person at this level of moral reasoning clings to a childhood perspective that survival depends primarily on *getting* rather than *giving*. Children often believe that in order to survive, they must get others to serve them, love them, and give to them. Such a perspective, however, places them in very dependent, insecure positions in their relationships.

Those who are able to achieve higher levels of moral reasoning have accepted childhood's end and more easily make the transition from a getting to a giving orientation.

Stage 3: Peer Pressure

In Stage 3, moral values are based primarily on living up to the expectations of others; their values become yours. At this stage, you think and behave as you believe your peers would think or behave in a given situation. For instance, if someone you know lied to his spouse about how much he paid for something, you might conclude it would be all right for you to do the same.

Stage 4: The Letter of the Law

In Stage 4, you begin to think and behave according to established authority; moral reasoning is very rigid and inflexible. Characterizing this stage are statements such as these: "I believe it because it says so right here in the Bible." "I don't make the rules, I just obey them." "You have to do it because I said so."

When operating at this stage, spouses may confront each other with what they perceive as the other's "duty" as a husband or wife. They may become defiant: "In this state, the law says everything is split fifty-fifty, and that means *everything*—including income!" "It's your responsibility to make enough money to feed and clothe this family, not mine." "Look, I give you $400 a month to buy groceries. It's your job to make it stretch far enough to feed the five of us for the entire month. My mother was able to feed six on less than that."

Living by "the letter of the law" shows some progress in the development of moral reasoning. But, as the above examples show, doing so still keeps one in the realm of self and does not necessarily foster concern for the feelings and welfare of others.

To form relationships with others is one of the most basic of human needs. We need others in order to gain greater security, create another generation, and expand our ideas and perspectives. Unfortunately, conflict can often develop between our need for emotional security and our need for financial security, and this can have a profound effect on our relationships. For example, some people marry primarily for love, others for money.

Stage 5: The Contract

In Stage 5 you base your moral reasoning on a more cooperative, unselfish interpretation of rules, regulations, and standards. At this level you are willing to enter into a "contract" with another person that you pledge to keep. While there are legal and financial factors to consider, your willingness to honor your agreement is a matter of self-respect and personal integrity. In taking out a loan, for example, you give your word that you will pay back the money you have borrowed. Even if you had to declare bankruptcy someday, you would still make every effort to pay back each creditor in full. It might take many years, and it might be very difficult financially, but you would intend to honor your commitment and preserve your good name.

The need to honor your commitments is especially true with regard to interpersonal relationships. In some relationships, commitment can extend to an agreement to allow unlimited access to your resources, even when it's inconvenient. In a relationship based on this kind of commitment, you have consented, by word or deed, to be used (not exploited, which means to be used without your consent). In this type of relationship, you are saying, "When you are hungry, use my food. When you have no place to go, use my place. When you are lonely, use me as a companion. After all, you are my friend."

Of course, to avoid a one-sided drain on your resources, this agreement must be mutual and reciprocal between the partners involved. In addition, the person being granted unlimited access to your resources must remain sensitive to the emotional and financial price you pay in order to honor your commitment. An example of this kind of commitment is illustrated in Hilda and Hector's relationship.

One day Hilda approached her husband, Hector, with an excited description of a beautiful blouse she had seen in a store window. "The one you said would look so terrific on me," Hilda exclaimed, "is on sale!"

Hector put his arm around her and cautioned, "On sale or not, we really can't afford it."

Hilda was thoughtful for a moment. Then, remembering the jar where Hector put his loose change each night, she asked, "Couldn't we use some of the money in your change jar?"

At first he protested, reminding her that he was saving the money for a computer program he had wanted for some time. But after a moment of reflecting and seeing the anticipation and excitement in her face, Hector smiled and agreed to use the money to buy the blouse. As she was leaving for the store, he called out jokingly, "You owe me one."

Months later, Hilda surprised Hector with a small package containing the computer program he had wanted.

Stage 6: The Golden Rule

If your moral reasoning has developed to Stage 6, your moral values are based on universal principles of compassion and mutual trust and respect for humanity. You recognize the dignity and worth of others, and your moral reasoning is founded on one of the oldest, simplest moral principles of all, the Golden Rule. At this stage, you treat others well, the way that you would like to be treated, simply because they are *human* and not because of their sex, race, age, wealth, social status, or relationship to you. You treat them as you would want to be treated.

You base a relationship on the Golden Rule if your first priority is a willingness to be charitable, to give without expectation of reciprocation. When you are charitable, you consider the needs of others to be at least as important as your own.

Jan and Satoshi have such a relationship. Jan had been accepted to a university but would receive only a partial scholarship toward her tuition. She and Satoshi were already working as much as they could, but they still had very little money. Things did not look too promising, and Jan was feeling discouraged. Suddenly, Satoshi burst into the room waving a check. "What do you have there?" she asked.

"Enough to make up for what your scholarship doesn't cover."

In a state of disbelief, Jan hesitantly asked, "But where—where did you get that kind of money?"

Satoshi had sold his car—the one he had dreamed of owning for several years. With tears quickly forming in her eyes, Jan threw her arms around his neck and softly told him, "Oh, how I love you. Thank you. Thank you so much." Then she leaned back and asked,

"How can I ever repay you?" Satoshi looked at her and replied, "By studying hard!"

The desire to be charitable stems from our ability to feel what others feel, recalling times when we were the ones who received help. Charity follows the same principle that governs sharing food at the dinner table: take some and pass it on.

Values and the Exchange of Resources

Far too many people in today's world seem to believe that the amount of money spent on them represents how much they are loved. Many a hardworking parent, bending from the pressure of such a belief, will combine money and affection in ways that further aggravate the family's already difficult financial situation.

Social scientist Uriel Foa proposes an economic model (see Figure 3.1, page 60) explaining some of the difficulties families face when trying to exchange certain resources.[2] Some resources are concrete, some symbolic; we care very much about who gives us some things (they are associated with a particular person), very little about who gives us other things (they have a universal value). Foa shows in his model why an exchange of related resources (such as love and service) is more likely to be effective than an exchange of unrelated resources (such as love and money).

Money can be easily exchanged for goods, for example, but attempts to exchange money for love are likely to fail. Gifts (goods), being a little closer to love, might be a more effective exchange. But exchanging thoughtfulness and consideration (service) for love is most likely to succeed.

Acting Responsibly and Being Considerate

To manage finances successfully within a relationship, a couple must achieve a balance between *acting responsibly* and *being considerate.* To act responsibly is to satisfy your needs and obligations without interfering with the ability of others to satisfy theirs. To be considerate is to have a genuine concern for the feelings and welfare of others.

Figure 3.2 (page 60) illustrates the four possible combinations of these two characteristics and their opposites, as well as the emotional results of these combinations. Examples of these combinations follow.

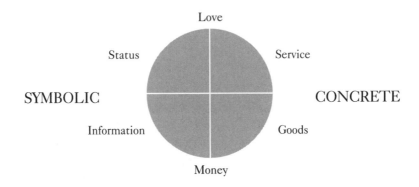

PARTICULARISTIC

Love

Status   Service

SYMBOLIC   CONCRETE

Information   Goods

Money

UNIVERSALISTIC

Figure 3.1. Resource exchange model. Adapted from Foa, 1971. Copyright (c) 1971 by the AAAS. Reprinted by permission.

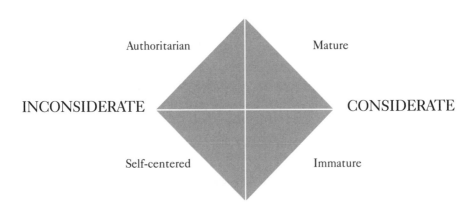

RESPONSIBLE

Authoritarian   Mature

INCONSIDERATE   CONSIDERATE

Self-centered   Immature

IRRESPONSIBLE

Figure 3.2 Possible combinations of the characteristics **responsible** and **considerate** (and their opposites) and the effects of these patterns on a relationship.

Considerate but Irresponsible

You are considerate but irresponsible when you think about the needs of others but are careless of the consequences of your actions. For instance, a husband buys his wife the new 21-gear mountain bike she wanted (considerate) at a time when they cannot even make the rent payments (irresponsible). As a consequence, the wife will most likely feel frustrated rather than pleased, because the husband has acted irresponsibly.

Tom is a prime example of this kind of behavior. In pleading with his wife, Carol, he said, "I've bought you everything that money can buy, and you still don't act like you really love me. What do you want from me?" These are the desperate words from someone trying to buy love.

Carol tried once again to explain to him that although she appreciated his gifts, they were gifts they could not afford. She told him that to be considerate, he didn't have to buy her *things*. Unfortunately, to this day, Tom still insists on buying gifts for her.

This example demonstrates that people can give money a symbolic meaning. Tom's gifts are intended to symbolize his love for Carol. But from Carol's perspective, his gifts symbolize how irresponsible he is. Until they can talk openly about the feelings behind their actions—and reactions—harmony between them will be impossible.

Irresponsible and Inconsiderate

When you don't care about possible consequences or about someone else's feelings, you are irresponsible and inconsiderate. For example, one spouse may be angry with the other and decide to get even by "maxing out" the credit cards on a spending spree. The couple has no way of paying off the debt, and could possibly face bankruptcy (irresponsible). It does not matter to the angry spouse how the other may feel about the spending spree (inconsiderate). After all, in this person's view, the other deserved it. In such cases, the "punished" spouse will usually feel angry and hurt because the other is self-centered. This is similar to the situation Marquita faced when she discovered that her husband had been deceiving her.

Marquita believed for years that economic fluctuations in Juan's business dealings affected his commissions. Not until she received a call from a salesman who worked with Juan did she learn of his gambling habits. The salesman had loaned Juan a considerable amount of money to cover some of his gambling debts and wanted her to influence Juan to repay him.

Marquita felt betrayed. When she confronted Juan about his gambling debts, he became angry and defensive. "Listen, what I do with *my* money is *my* business. I doubt I'll hear you complaining if I come home with some big winnings. So stay off my case while I'm in a slump."

Marquita felt as though she didn't really know the man she was married to. She wondered how else she had been deceived and whether her whole marriage was a sham. She also wondered whether she would ever be able to trust Juan again.

Habitual gamblers have a tendency to lose it all. Being irresponsible and inconsiderate usually leads to financial disaster *and* the destruction of relationships.

Responsible and Inconsiderate

As the head of the household, you may act responsibly simply because someone has to pay the bills and put food on the table. But because of the stress associated with these tasks, you may find yourself being inconsiderate of your family's feelings. Because of excessive debt, for example, you may decide to take a second job (responsible) without recognizing how your spouse and children might feel about not being able to spend time together as a family (inconsiderate). You also may end up irritable and unpleasant because of stress and exhaustion.

Family members may voice their complaints about not seeing you as much, but you tell them that you would not have to work so much if they would just turn off the lights and turn down the thermostat. Even though you are "doing it all for them," they may feel insignificant, and you will be seen as authoritarian. Samuel provides a good example of the consequences that result from being overly responsible and woefully inconsiderate.

One evening Samuel got upset about the family's chronic indebtedness and criticized his wife, Sarah, for not showing more restraint in spending. Waving an unpaid bill at her, Samuel shouted accusingly, "You act as if money grew on trees. You're spending it faster than I can make it."

Sarah responded defensively, "I've cut back on everything I can think of short of making underwear out of old pillowcases. I'm not sure what more I can do to help."

Without thinking, Samuel retorted, "If you really want to help out around here, get a job and start bringing in some money so we can pay off these debts."

Responsible and Considerate

When you are acting responsibly and being considerate of your partner's feelings, chances are good that you will achieve success in both your financial and personal life. Assume, for instance, that you want to withdraw funds from your savings account in order to gain what you think would be a higher return on an investment. However, being sensitive to your partner's need for a feeling of security, you first ask how he or she would feel about such a decision. In this situation, your spouse would most likely feel loved and see you as mature and caring.

Martha and Kirk have such a relationship, and when it came time to decide what to do with Kirk's Christmas bonus, being responsible and considerate really paid off. Martha thought it would be wiser to spend the $1,000 bonus on debts than to put it into savings. "It's going to take us until March or April to pay off our Visa card," she told Kirk, "but if we use the bonus money, we could pay most of it off right away. What would you like to do with the bonus?"

Kirk is concerned about how well the company he works for will perform during the upcoming year. "I know how you feel about being in debt and paying all that interest," he said, "but I'm a little worried about possible layoffs. I'd like to put at least some of it into savings. How about if we were to put $500 on the credit card and the other $500 into savings?"

NOTES

1. Kohlberg, 1963, 1969.
2. Foa, 1971.

CHAPTER 4

COMMUNICATION AND INTIMACY

Good communication is crucial to effective money management. Communication cannot be accomplished alone; at least two people must interact to create communication. When we have trouble communicating, it is not the fault of just one person. Bad communication happens because of the interaction process. For communication to improve, all involved parties need to take responsibility for their contributions.

Circular Communication Systems

While we often think of events and their causes as linear (A causes B), this is often not true in the context of relationships. With people influencing each other as they interact, causality is often circular: Person A's actions influence person B's, B's influence C's, C's influence D's, which in turn may influence A's (see Figure 4.1).

The following interaction sequence, an example of the circular model of causality, might occur in a family:

A. The mother is having an argument with the father over their daughter's behavior and, during the course of the argument, the mother begins to withdraw.

B. The father, frustrated by the withdrawal, begins to yell.

C. The daughter begins to cry.

D. The father becomes more frustrated and yells louder.

E. The daughter cries harder.

F. The mother defends the daughter.

G. The daughter, holding on to her mother, cries more.

H. The father withdraws by stomping out of the room.

I. The mother begins to yell at the father—and where it stops, nobody knows.

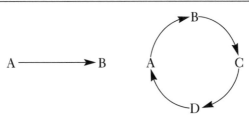

Figure 4.1. *Two models of causality.*

In this illustration, father, mother, and daughter have developed a system of interaction in which each influences the behavior of the other. However, since each person is part of the cycle that perpetuates the pattern, there is no single "cause" for the mother's or the father's withdrawal or for their yelling. Systems such as this usually resist change. The pattern seeks to maintain a familiar state of equilibrium, and each person plays a part in the process.

If you have ever found yourself thinking *Here we go again* or *We've been over all this before*, then you have encountered a circular-communication system. To achieve a different pattern, at least one participant needs to change his or her part in the cycle.

Changing the System

Family rules guide the characteristics of particular circular-communication systems. In the example above, one rule is that the mother will defend the daughter. The mother may or may not be aware that such a rule operates in her family, but her behavior is nevertheless governed by it. For this communication system to change, at least one participant needs to behave differently. One individual's change will influence changes in other individuals.

For example, if the father were to stop yelling, the pattern would change, and the daughter might be influenced to try something besides crying. If the daughter didn't cry but negotiated instead, the mother would no longer have a reason to play her familiar "protector" role in the pattern. Instead, the mother might choose to talk to the father about what's bothering him. The father would not "cause" these changes by altering his behavior. Instead, by changing *his part* in the system (or changing a rule that governed his behavior), the system would adjust to his change in ways he could not predict.

Be aware that such changes in family communication rules are often difficult to make. Frequently, when one person breaks out and tries something different, other family members try, either overtly or covertly, to bring the "wayward" member back so that the old, familiar balance can be maintained.

Perpetuating the System

Continuing this example, let's say that the daughter leaves her family to marry. Her marital-communication system will likely be different from her family's system, but she may try to perpetuate some of her old, familiar patterns. If her husband should yell at her for some reason, she may initially break down and cry, hoping that someone (possibly her mother) will take her side. If the daughter's husband comes from a family in which people tend to yell back and then later apologize, he may be confused or even hurt by his wife's behavior.

In this example, family communication rules conflict (see chapter 2). The daughter is following the rule "When someone yells at me, I cry and go find help." The husband is following the rule "After I yell at someone, they yell back, but then we both need to apologize." The difference between these rules is likely to leave both spouses wondering what to do next.

Because these household rules are not written and hung on the refrigerator, the partners may not understand that they are operating from different, unstated patterns. This conflict is not "caused" by either spouse acting independently of the other. They interact and influence each other's behavior in a circular way.

The "Dance"

Francine shakes an accusing finger at Ralph and critically points out, "Whenever I try to talk to you about finances, you just get mad and stomp off." Ralph counters, "Well, you usually throw the checkbook at me, and tell me that if I'm so smart I can balance it myself." Both Ralph and Francine would probably agree on at least one thing: they have a problem talking about finances.

The communication pattern between Ralph and Francine can be compared to a dance. Any two people who have been together for an extended period of time tend to develop interaction patterns. These patterns are like dance steps, and, like dance partners, spouses get used to responding to each other in certain ways. The "dance" involves both parties, and both are responsible for the patterns they have created. If a certain "dance step" isn't working, both partners have the power to choose new steps. When one spouse takes a different step, the partner has an opportunity to respond differently. Even small changes on the part of one or both provide opportunities to create new patterns and to improve the relationship:

1. Katya, looking frustrated, complains loudly, "This checkbook is a mess."

Boris complains back, "Ha! You've got no room to be criticizing me for the way *I* keep a checkbook."

"Look who's talking," Katya responds. "Your biggest problem is that you can't take constructive criticism."

"That's because you never know what you're talking about," Boris snaps.

"You never listen to me long enough to know," Katya says. "I think it's a trait that runs in your family. You're just like your mother."

"*My* mother? If we're on the subject of mothers, let's talk about *your* mother."

Each spouse continues to respond without attempting to understand the problem. The "dance steps" center on blame and irrelevant issues that hurt.

2. Katya says, "This checkbook is a mess."

Boris, looking over her shoulder, responds, "What's the problem?"

With frustration in her voice, Katya continues, "I sat down to balance our checking account and noticed that nothing was recorded for check number 728. Do you remember when it was written?"

"Sure," Boris answers. "It was last Thursday when I took the kids to the doctor. I was so involved with how high their fevers were and how pale they looked that I just wrote out a check to the receptionist and bundled them back into the car."

Katya smiles knowingly. "It sounds like you had your hands full."

Boris smiles back and nods. "It was like trying to keep puppies in a box."

Each spouse has attempted to understand and support the other—and the content of their discussion remains relevant to the problem.

Today's world is filled with the pressures of too many things to do and not enough time to do them. Mistakes are bound to happen. Our ability to look past the mistakes to see the effort put forth by another in our behalf allows us to be empathetic rather than critical.

Communication that Works

The Communication Goals Exercise

Take some time during the next week to look at your communication patterns and the responses you make to the "dance" that you and your spouse perform. Write your observations on the Communication Goals Exercise, Worksheet 4.1 (page 79).

The Zap Rule

To become more aware of problems caused by ineffective communication patterns, you may also want to employ the "zap rule." The zap rule is a tool to help you communicate more effectively, letting you know when you have said something hurtful or demeaning, and giving you a chance to express the same idea in a more loving, supportive way.

A *zap* is anything that makes you feel as if you're not being treated as an equal or with dignity and respect, or as if you are being blamed, punished, or ridiculed. The zap rule requires that the conversation stop immediately when you or your spouse perceives a zap, and that the offending party rephrase the comment. This is how it works:

1. When you feel you have been *zapped,* raise your hand or stop the discussion.

2. Tell the other person, *in a non-accusatory way,* that you felt zapped. You need not justify your feelings. The zapped person is

assumed to be right; therefore, the zapping person should not attempt to convince the other that the comment wasn't really a zap.

3. Ask the zapping person to rephrase the statement, or modify the tone of voice used to express the statement so as to remove its zap characteristics. ("Would you like to paraphrase that?")

4. The zapping person should attempt to rephrase the comment so that the zap is removed.

5. Thank the person for rephrasing.

6. Only three zaps are allowed per discussion. If more than three zaps occur, take time out from that particular topic (at least thirty minutes), but agree to come back to it later.

Levels of Communication

One of the most common sources of dissatisfaction in communication results from partners expressing themselves on different levels of intimacy. For example, after an evening of dinner and dancing, one spouse says, "I had a good time tonight. Getting out like that really means a lot to me." The other spouse responds on a different level of intimacy: "The music was okay, but I thought the price of dinner was outrageous. We could feed the whole family for a week on what it cost us tonight." The first spouse is communicating on a *feeling* level while the second is communicating on a *cognitive* level. The most effective communication occurs when both partners communicate on the same level.

In *Dynamics of Personal Adjustment*, Harold Bernard and Wesley Huckins discuss five levels of communication.[1] Each level has its own combination of content, meaning, and emotional involvement, and each level can play an important part in discussing finances.

Level 5: Clichés and Greetings

Level 5 is the least intimate level of communication. You use this level in casual conversations. It includes greetings and clichés such as "How are you?" and "Money just seems to burn a hole in my pocket."

Level 4: Information and Directions

You use Level 4 primarily to give directions and exchange information. Financially compatible couples inform each other of pertinent details: "I stopped by the bank today. The reason our checkbook doesn't balance is that we're not recording our automatic teller withdrawals."

Level 3: Feelings about External Events

Level 3 is the first level at which you express individual feelings, but only about the *external* world. You may share likes and dislikes, and feelings associated with values, attitudes, and beliefs. You may say, for example, "I hate going into debt as much as you do, but how else can we afford to get the car repaired unless we put it on a credit card?"

Level 2: Feelings about Internal Events

Using Level 2, you attempt to express emotions on a deeper level—that of your *internal* world—what is going on inside you rather than outside you. At this level, you may express high-risk feelings such as love, loneliness, and hurt. You might tell your spouse, "I have never felt so unloved, so unimportant as when I saw you drive up in that new car. I pleaded with you not to buy it, not to bury us further in debt. For a moment I actually hated you."

Level 1: Intuition

Level 1 is the most intimate level of communication. On this level, you communicate a sense of oneness and togetherness. In contrast to the other levels, this level is usually nonverbal. Because of the intensity of emotions, communication often takes place through eye contact, embrace, and touch. Children are very good at interpreting this level of communication. When giving someone a gift, children will immediately look at the recipient's face to evaluate how the person *really* feels about the gift. They seem to know intuitively that most of what we communicate is nonverbal.

In general, 95 percent of what we communicate is nonverbal (tone of voice, gestures, posture, facial expressions, personal possessions, and so forth), while only 5 percent is verbal (words). When verbal and nonverbal messages contradict each other, we tend to believe that the nonverbal is the more truthful message.

The Importance of Communicating on a Feeling Level

Unfortunately, many married couples seem to spend most of their time trying to communicate on levels 5 (clichés) and 4 (information), which keeps their relationship on a fairly superficial level. For greater intimacy, couples must communicate as much as possible on the feeling levels (levels 3, 2, and 1).

You are responsible for your willingness to commit to a relationship, to risk being vulnerable, and to express your feelings openly and honestly. You are responsible for what communication you send to your partner, and for interpreting what you receive. But you are *not* responsible for how your partner receives what you send. Rather, your partner (the receiver) should tell you (the sender) what the communication *represents* to him or her and then ask you whether that was your *intent*.

After putting the kids to bed, Jeff returns to the kitchen to confront his wife, Pat. "When you told me that you had already paid this month's bills, I felt like a complete failure. It came across as if you wanted to take over because I was doing a lousy job. Is that what you really think?"

Pat, with a look of surprise at such an accusation, replies, "For heaven's sake, no. I think you're doing a fine job paying the bills. But I know how time-consuming and upsetting paying the bills can be, and I thought that since your final exams were at the beginning of the month, I'd save you the time and frustration by paying them for you."

Communicating on the feeling levels is especially important when you deal with what each partner *expects* from the relationship compared to what each *receives*. Most relationships that fail are built on promises that cannot be kept, and on expectations that cannot be met. When someone promises to *make* someone else happy, the person to whom the promise was made expects to be made happy. When that person becomes miserable, guess who gets the blame?

One love-struck individual may say, "I've been miserable all my life," and the other replies, "So have I." In unison they exclaim, "Let's get married and make each other happy!" If one of the spouses is not happy later, that spouse may assume that the other is withholding the "happy power." This assumption, of course, releases the unhappy one from personal responsibility for the current state of affairs.

In many cases, happiness is associated with being something, doing something, or having something. Happiness can result from being important to someone, or from feeling special or irreplaceable. It can come from having your feelings appreciated or having consideration given to your need to do something or have something. In the latter case, however, "happy power" can often translate into financial power. If you think you can meet your spouse's needs and yet selfishly withhold resources—depriving your spouse of activities or things that bring happiness—you are misusing your power and are likely leaving your partner disillusioned with the marriage.

Negotiations

One of the most effective ways of meeting each other's needs within a relationship is through the process of *negotiation*. Negotiation is a cooperative decision-making process in which two or more parties talk in an effort to resolve their differences. The primary purpose of negotiating is to achieve agreement; the secondary purpose is to establish and maintain long-term relationships. As with building a house, building a marriage requires a willingness to negotiate and compromise to reach mutually satisfying solutions.

Negotiating is an essential part of everyday life; the better you become at it, the more often you can peaceably settle misunderstandings, including financial problems. You can avoid many of the problems associated with meeting needs within relationships, as well as some of those you encounter when dealing with creditors, by using basic negotiation guidelines.[2]

First of all, know that negotiations are *not* intended to be win-lose battles but a means of arriving at solutions that are *mutually beneficial*. To avoid developing a win-lose mentality, you must separate the *people* from the *problem*. Remember that you want to attack your financial problem, not each other. One of the first things you need to negotiate is how you are going to treat each other. From the first encounter, you should make every effort to ease tensions, safeguard your partner's self-esteem, and show appropriate consideration for his or her position.

When negotiating, if one person insists on "winning it all," that person will ultimately lose in terms of the relationship. The parties involved are *opponents who need each other*, and must be able to treat each other with dignity—something that is especially important in family negotiations. The dignity with which a member of the family is treated during past negotiations has a major impact on how willing that person will be to negotiate future impasses. No one should ever be left with feelings of resentment or defeat.

Pre-negotiation Planning

A number of factors contribute to successful negotiations. One of the most essential is pre-negotiation planning, which should include at least the following:

1. Know what you want and what the other person wants.

2. Know what is negotiable and what is not.

3. Establish priorities; know the relative importance of various items to be negotiated.

4. Know what you are willing to give up.

5. Acquire the necessary facts and information about each issue or item.

6. Develop a reasonable defense for your position.

7. Develop alternatives.

The Opening Proposal

The opening proposal should be realistic and show some consideration for the opposing position. It should also be credible—the other person must believe you are sincere. The degree of sincerity you project depends a great deal on your reputation: In the past, have you been ethical, fulfilled commitments, and acted expeditiously?

After you make the opening proposal, be prepared to settle for less than you expected. If negotiations result in more than you expected, you will be pleasantly surprised. But you will never get more than you ask for *originally*, so open a little high. The positions you take later may then appear more reasonable or generous, and you will be able to give up more during the process. In this way, the "give and take" principle can more easily work, and the other person is more likely to make a greater number of counterproposals.

Making Concessions

Making a concession means changing your offer in favor of the other party. The change reduces the benefits you are seeking and encourages the other party to either come to an agreement or make a concession in exchange. Keep in mind that the fact your opponent has agreed to negotiate is a sign of readiness to make concessions. Look for areas of common interest and solutions that might benefit both parties.

Keep your concessions small and infrequent. Your first concession should be your largest, and each subsequent concession should be smaller than the previous one. For example, if you are negotiating a selling price, you might propose a price of $200 and then make a $30 concession, bringing the price down to $170. For your next concession, though, you should come down only $20, and only $10 for your third concession. Meanwhile, the buyer will increase offers by a similar progression. As a consequence, both the seller and the buyer will soon be able to project an optimal, mutually satisfying price.

Similarly, when negotiating the distribution of financial responsibilities within a relationship, you might open with "I'll pay two of the fixed bills," followed by a proposal to pay four of the fixed bills but none of the variable bills. Later, you might concede to pay all the fixed bills and two of the variables.

Counterproposals

Before making a counter proposal, review what has already been proposed and evaluate how your counteroffer can serve a *common good*. Above all, do not phrase your counterproposal as a threat. If someone has made a concession in good faith, for example, do not reciprocate with an ultimatum: "You'd better come up with something better than that or I'm walking out of here," or "Carrying just one check with you and leaving the rest at home may work, but if you bounce one more check, your name is coming off the account, and that's final!"

Reaching an Agreement

Remember that your ultimate objective is to arrive at a mutually acceptable agreement, not to get the other person to let you have your way. If you are willing to lower initial demands, make frequent concessions, and consider the interests of the other person, you can greatly improve your chances of reaching an agreement.

Sometimes negotiations become *deadlocked*—neither side is willing to move from a particular position. Perhaps attitudes have become hostile because feelings have been needlessly hurt, or past experiences have contributed to an atmosphere of distrust. When this happens, apologies are generally the most effective way to end the deadlock.

Closing

Closing a negotiation becomes possible when both parties have achieved most of their objectives. For instance, a creditor hoping to receive immediately 100 percent of what was owed may settle for 80 percent in three equal installments. Or one spouse, who had hoped to avoid paying bills alone, may succeed in convincing the other spouse to assume responsibility for the fixed-payment debts. In both cases, the negotiations will have closed successfully.

Sometimes you can close by proposing an overall final offer that ties smaller items into one cohesive package. Such a proposal is usually made when one party perceives that the other has made all the concessions he or she is willing to make. Then, as an incentive to close, a package of special concessions is included. For example, one spouse may propose, "I'm willing to do it all: pay the bills, write the creditors, and do the shopping for one month while you study for your entrance exams, if in return you will use the extra time for studying and nothing else."

Closing can also take place when a solution is proposed that is unique and simple, yet substantially different from the alternatives that have already been suggested: "Rather than arguing over whether you or I should manage the finances, why don't we hire an accountant to do it?"

Once you reach an agreement, record the details in writing and *do not try to make any changes.* Try to maintain a sense of acceptance toward the outcome, and avoid thinking about what you might have done or said differently. Above all, try to view both sides as victorious.

Reframing

The real success of negotiations lies in how each person chooses to interpret the outcome. In many cases, it is far easier for us to change our perspective than to change someone else's behavior. The process of changing perspectives is called *reframing.* Family therapist Paul Watzlawick believes that by *reframing*—changing one's conceptual or emotional point of view on an event—family members can gain greater understanding of family processes.[3]

John Milton, in *Paradise Lost*, provided us with perhaps the most poetic definition of reframing:

> The mind is its own place, and in itself
> Can make a heaven of hell, a hell of heaven.[4]

Milton's view suggests that it is we who, through our ability to interpret the world in a variety of ways, determine the way we see the world around us.

Amanda was feeling frustrated and angry over the fact that her father was putting 15 percent of his paycheck into savings every month. She felt the family needed at least some of that money for clothes and entertainment. Her father, however, was adamant and would not consider saving any less.

Amanda saw her father as stingy and mean, and she doubted that he really loved her and the other children. But when she talked with her father, he revealed that when he was a child, his family had gone through the Great Depression. Having witnessed the agony and trials that his parents, brothers, and sisters had gone through, he had vowed that when he grew up he would make sure that this kind of hardship would never befall his family. Reframing her father's behavior within the context of his experience with the Depression enabled Amanda to see his saving money as an act of love and concern for the family rather than as an act of selfishness.

Reframing can also be helpful when you try to communicate feelings about a particular purchase. The concept of *meaningful units*, as discussed in chapter 1, is an example of reframing. The cost of a pair of shoes was one couple's meaningful unit. The partners were able to arrive at the relative value of other wants by appraising how many pairs of shoes they could buy with the amount paid for other items. A new garbage disposal, for example, cost six pairs of shoes, cable TV cost two pairs of shoes a month, and one month's supply of soft drinks cost four pairs.

The relative-value information provided by meaningful units is often more useful than knowing an item's cost in money alone. With an increased understanding of each other's values, a couple can achieve an even greater level of sensitivity and intimacy.

Notes

1. Bernard and Huckins, 1975, 330–37.
2. Poduska, 1987.
3. Watzlawick, Weakland, and Fisch, 1974.
4. Milton, *Paradise Lost.*

WORKSHEET 4.1—COMMUNICATION GOALS EXERCISE

Decide independently of each other what communication goals you and your spouse would like to achieve. After you complete your separate lists, select and discuss three goals you hold in common. (The common goals may be chosen from the individual goals, or they may be some combination of the individual goals.)

I would like to see us achieve these three communication goals:

1. _____

2. _____

3. _____

My spouse would like to see us achieve these three communication goals:

1. _____

2. _____

3. _____

These are the three communication goals we have in common that we would like to achieve:

1. _____

2. _____

3. _____

PART 2

Your Financial Past, Present, and Future

One reason most budgets simply do not work is that they are developed around a time frame that is too limiting. Budgets often focus on the current month only, as if what happens during *that* month portrays the entire financial picture. This restricted view inhibits the development of a successful financial management program. To achieve a truly effective budgeting process, you must work with three different, but interrelated, time frames.

First, take a look at your financial *past* to better understand how you got where you are today, and how to cope effectively with your debt load. Next, look toward the *future* to get some idea of how to avoid budget-sabotaging "eight balls" that always seem to come along just when you think you are getting your finances under control. Dealing with the future also includes making plans for retirement, insurance, and education. It is important to decide where you eventually want to be financially, what kind of effort you will need to make in order to get there, and how much time you will need.

After you have a better understanding of how the past and the future can affect your current situation, you will be ready to begin managing your budget in the *present.*

CHAPTER **5**

UNDERSTANDING WHY YOU
HAVE FINANCIAL PROBLEMS

It is important to explore your past as you attempt to understand what behavior has been responsible for your current financial situation. Major considerations in this chapter are two principles from chapter 1—Principle 1: *Financial problems are usually behavior problems rather than money problems;* Principle 2: *If you continue doing what you are doing, you will continue getting what you are getting.*

If you find yourself saying, "I've been trying to get out of debt for the past twelve years, but I haven't made it yet," then you are most likely set in a pattern of *behavior* that perpetuates chronic indebtedness. According to Principle 2, you will have to change what you have been doing or you will continue in debt for the rest of your life.

How Did You Get into This Mess?

We get into financial messes for many reasons. Some reasons are beyond our control, but most stem from our emotions—impatience, envy, anger, love, craving, inadequacy, insecurity, and loneliness. For example, the interest you pay on a loan is often the cost of impatience, the "I want it, and I want it now" syndrome. Impatience can be a very expensive emotion, and so can others. It may be wise to consider the adage "*Impatience* is trying to make things occur on *our* schedule while *patience* is accepting that things will occur on *God's* schedule."

The following list of questions indicates some of the reasons people get into financial messes. Try to identify the emotions associated with each type of behavior—and which behaviors most closely match your own.

1. Do you buy items that are usually associated with a higher socioeconomic level than your income warrants? Do you compete with someone else or with a particular comparison group? Do you buy things to compensate for feelings of inadequacy or because of a need to impress others? This behavior is identified as *trying to move too far, too fast.*

2. Do you habitually live beyond your means, and are any anticipated increases in income already committed? Do you buy into "get-rich-quick" schemes or high-risk investments? Does your financial plan lack emergency funds or savings programs? This behavior is identified as *failure to determine what is sufficient.*

3. Do you *lack basic financial management skills?*

4. Do you have a history of *impulse buying?* Have you been self-indulgent in an attempt to compensate for loneliness or the feeling that no one cares about you?

5. When you buy something, do you neglect to take into account the hidden, indirect, and relationship costs? This is identified as *failure to determine the true cost of a purchase.*

6. Do you buy things that you use infrequently and that you could have rented for much less? This is called *failure to analyze the cost per use.*

7. Do you *lack sufficient medical or liability insurance coverage?*

8. Are you staggering under your debt load? This may be because of *credit abuse.*

9. Do you have *addictive behaviors*, such as gambling, hoarding, or substance abuse (alcohol, illegal drugs, nicotine, prescription drugs)?

Trying to Move Too Far, Too Fast

Most of us live in an upwardly mobile society; however, the pace at which we attempt to move from one socioeconomic level to another can have a dramatic impact on our financial situation. For the sake of simplicity, assume that there are only five socioeconomic levels and that these levels can be identified primarily by the amount of income earned and the types of purchases made, as shown in Table 5.1.

TABLE 5.1—SOCIOECONOMIC LEVELS AND TYPES OF PURCHASES

SOCIOECONOMIC LEVEL	ANNUAL INCOME	BOAT PURCHASE	HOUSING
5. High	$100,000+	Yacht	Mansion
4. Medium high	$50–99,000	Cruiser	Large house
3. Medium	$30–49,000	21-foot inboard	Medium house
2. Medium low	$15–29,000	12-foot outboard	Small house
1. Low	below $15,000	Canoe	Rental unit

Purchasing items corresponding to your level of income is possible, although it usually means saving for a while first. Buying items corresponding to a lower level of income than your own usually means paying cash and being able to buy immediately. For example, if your income were around $45,000 per year and you wished to buy a 21-foot inboard powerboat—a purchase within your income level—you would have to save for a while, but the boat would be attainable. If you wanted to buy a 12-foot outboard—a purchase within a *lower* income level—you could probably pay cash for it without having to save. But if you were to attempt to purchase a cruiser (a boat that has a bathroom)—which corresponds to a *higher* socioeconomic level—you would have to go into debt to buy it.

Financial problems are inevitable when you try to move too far, too fast, and begin to consume at a rate that exceeds your current level of income. The remedy is simple: To avoid unnecessary debt, *make purchases that are appropriate to your income level.* To help you become converted to this fundamental principle, consider the following issues.

Assets and Liabilities

For the most part, debt is a symptom of trying to live beyond your means—trying to obtain status symbols that are beyond your level of income. It's like going to a bank and explaining, "I'm going to be honest with you loan officers. I cannot possibly live the lifestyle I want to live or buy the things I'd like to buy unless you agree to contribute thousands of dollars toward making my dreams come true. It's obvious that I cannot afford to live in the manner to which I would like to become accustomed on my current salary. So how about it? Do I get the loan?"

You need to realize that, in actuality, your *equity* is your contribution toward maintaining your lifestyle; your *liabilities* are the contributions others make. Assume you—and the bank—buy a $10,000 car, for example. You must divide this asset into the portion you own and the portion the bank owns. Your $2,000 down payment represents your equity in the car. The loan you received from the bank ($8,000 paid to the dealer) counts as a liability.

The Cost of Belonging

"Buying up" is often an attempt to gain acceptance from those you admire. Trying to buy a sense of belonging can be very expensive, both directly and indirectly. Direct expenses are the costs of "membership" in the group. They might include joining a country club, spa, or private or professional organization, as well as purchasing privileged seating at sports, entertainment, or political events.

Indirect expenses come through other consumer practices, such as buying a house in a particular neighborhood. The make and model of the car you drive may represent an attempt to be included in a particular group, as may the logos on your clothes and shopping bags. Quite often, the indirect costs of membership in a social group are even higher than the direct costs.

Unfortunately, the truth of Principle 6—*You can never get enough of what you don't need because what you don't need can never satisfy you*—often defeats misguided efforts to buy acceptance and belonging. Spending to achieve a higher status, to control others, or to feel important is expensive and wasteful—and, for most, unaffordable. In the long run, such spending is futile and ungratifying, partly because of the inherent lack of intimacy associated with it, and partly because of the gradual development of a dependence on the things that money can buy.

Conspicuous Consumption

The need to impress others is often found in people who want to be accepted by those at a higher economic level and who, simultaneously, loathe being regarded as equals by their peers at a lower socioeconomic level. Pride and envy play a big part in their lives.

Prideful individuals engage in what is commonly referred to as *conspicuous consumption*—acquiring goods and services not because they are needed but because they are expensive, generate attention, and provide the appearance of affluence. Such individuals often see themselves as less successful than a particular group of high achievers and are constantly trying to catch up with them. In the process, they tend to "compare to lose": if they drive a Buick, they notice the Cadillac; if they are in a Cadillac, they want a Mercedes; if they drive a Mercedes, they compare themselves to Rolls Royce owners. Regardless of how high they climb, they inevitably lose in the comparison. Those in higher brackets see to that!

Self-Worth

Comparing oneself to others is counterproductive in another way: some of those who do so may feel like impostors when they finally achieve professional and financial success. They believe that others really deserve their successes, while they have just been lucky.[1] They fear that sooner or later their "secret" will be discovered, and others will find out that all the things they have surrounded themselves with were bought on credit and have no substance behind them.

Far too many people believe that their self-worth rests on the numbers found on their balance sheets rather than on the mutual respect found in their relationships. They believe that people are worth more if they have lots of money and are worth less if they don't. In most cases, people express their true self-worth by what they can *do*, even though they try to impress others by what they can *buy*. The need for belonging can be best satisfied through what people can *contribute*, not through what they can *consume* (Principle 10, chapter 1).

You may wish to explore your own beliefs by asking yourself these questions: How do I judge my own worth and that of others? What are my intentions when making purchases—to *express* my self-worth or to *impress* others with my financial worth?

Failure to Determine What Is Sufficient

When you buy a car, your main concerns are what you can afford and what would be *enough* car (how many of the amenities you can live without). But determining what would be enough income is more complex—you must decide whether you are referring to an *open-ended* or a *closed-ended* amount.

Open-ended versus Closed-ended Budgets

With an open-ended budget, you have not determined how much money is enough. No matter how much your current income is, you are probably thinking in terms of making more, and your budget is unrealistically based on anticipated increases in income. Take, for example, the words of this overly optimistic planner: "Can you believe that between the two of us we made over $52,000 last year? If we play our cards right, we ought to make at least $60,000 this year, and maybe $70,000 next year. The size of that new house is looking bigger and bigger. If it keeps going like this, it won't be long before we're talking about a pool and a sauna."

Aristotle, observing the people of his day in about 340 B.C., almost prophetically described the financial world that today's families face:

"Some persons are led to believe that getting wealth is the object of household management, and the whole idea of their lives is that they ought either to increase their money without limit, or at any rate not to lose it. The origin of this disposition in men is that they are intent upon living only, and not upon living well; and, as their desires are unlimited, they also desire that the means of gratifying them should be without limit."[2]

In contrast, when you consider a closed-ended budget, you have decided how much income you would consider *sufficient*. With the necessary income predetermined, you are in a position to regulate your expenditures accordingly and to experience the freedom that comes from living within your means. (Specific skills for accomplishing this are included in chapter 7.) For instance, if you determined that $30,000 per year was a sufficient income and adjusted your spending to that figure, then any additional income would be uncommitted and could be saved or spent as you see fit. Imagine the result: "I can't believe how much we have in savings already. Our decision to put half of every salary increase into savings and to use the other half to compensate for cost-of-living increases has worked out beautifully."

Open-ended budgeting—in other words, living beyond your

means and having any increases in income already committed—eventually leads to financial insecurity. It's like walking a tightrope—if you have no financial safety net, a fall will kill you. Nobody wants to live in a world that precarious.

Financial Security

To make your world a little safer, you must prepare for the unexpected. Financial planners recommend that an emergency savings fund of at least three months' expenses be maintained at all times. Unfortunately, too few people have such a savings program. And too many people have no savings program to provide them with sufficient retirement funds. As a result, many never achieve a feeling of financial security.

Just about everyone dreams of someday being financially secure. But since there are no guarantees in life, in most cases what we really achieve is a *feeling* of security rather than actual security. For example, many workers place large amounts of savings in pension funds, but because of poor management or fraud by others, the workers are left destitute. Money in a pension fund does not necessarily mean you are financially secure. It may mean that for the time being, you just *feel* financially secure.

Feelings of security or insecurity are generated as much by what is going on inside you as by what is happening outside of you. Internal threats, for the most part, come from a series of "what-ifs": What if I lose my job? What if I can't keep up the payments? What if I don't get the raise? Fortunately, most of these fears are seldom realized; nevertheless, the stress from the worry is very real. On the other hand, self-confidence results from knowing you *can* cope with whatever happens in life, rather than from futile attempts to control what *might* happen.

What Is Enough Home?

Included in the quest for security is the issue of safeguarding whatever we call home. Being able to pay the rent, build a house, or pay the mortgage is often paramount in maintaining a sense of well-being and security. Your security in your home is directly related to how your income compares with your expenses.

While most lending institutions recommend that home buyers

limit their mortgage liability to no more than 25 to 30 percent of their gross income, many people carry mortgage liabilities in excess of 50 percent of their income.

Attempting to impress others is often a major cause of excessive mortgage indebtedness. You may want to ask yourself, "How much of the house is for me and how much is for impressing others? If these 'others' were not involved, how much house would I really need?" Whether you are buying a home, renting an apartment, or leasing a condo, the primary questions are the same: "What is sufficient? What is enough house? Enough money? Enough security?"

It is helpful to establish a "goal alignment" between you and your spouse to determine what would be *sufficient* in your lives, regardless of what others have. Begin by separately listing what each would consider a sufficient income, house, car, and so on. Then share, negotiate, and compromise to make a mutual list of what it would take for both of you to be financially satisfied with your lives. The primary goal is to set limits on your needs and wants.

Lack of Budgeting and Management Skills

Over a lifetime, the average family will manage between $1.5 and $2 million ($35,000 to $50,000 per year for 40 years in current dollars). Imagine running a business that will gross a couple million dollars and deciding that it is not necessary to write anything down— "We'll just wing it." Far too often this is exactly what families do.

Most families have only a rough idea of where their money goes. They simply live from paycheck to paycheck, regardless of the paycheck's size. As long as the money keeps coming, or until something unexpected happens, all is well.

Most people have never been taught how to manage their money—only how to earn it. Such ignorance can mean losing in two minutes what it took you two weeks to earn. For example, you may be talking to a car dealer who has just shifted from "sales price" to "monthly payments." He tells you, "For just $10 a month more you can have the stripes, *and* for only an additional $5 a month you can have the tinted mirrors." If you say, "Hey, what's an extra $15? I'll take both!" you have just added $900 plus interest to the price of the car over a five-year contract ($15 x 60 monthly payments).

A more effective way of dealing with situations like the one just described is to use the concept of *analyzing marginal (or additional) costs*. Compare the amount of additional value you would receive to the money it would cost you to buy the extra items. For the above example, you would ask yourself if the addition of the stripes and tinted mirrors add an extra $900 to the value of the car. Or, considering your personal preferences and desires, would having these items on your car be worth $900 to you? In other words, would you be getting your money's worth? One of the ways to increase your chances of accurately answering this and other related questions is to take advantage of community educational resources such as libraries, schools, and seminars. The more financially educated you become and the more related skills you acquire, the closer you will come to financial wisdom and security.

Impulse Buying

Most phone solicitations and late-night TV "$19.95 plus shipping and handling" ads sell items few people would ever put on their shopping lists. So the manufacturers, in hopes of selling their products, bring them to the buyer. You have probably never made out a shopping list that included, for instance, time shares in an Icelandic condo, an inflatable raft with a battery-operated outboard motor (batteries not included), or a year's supply of avocado pits as a treatment for gout. But you just might buy such items on impulse. Similarly, most supermarkets place items that are least likely to be on your list at eye level or near the checkout stand to encourage you to buy on impulse.

For some people, buying things whenever they want them gives them a sense of power or control over their lives. For others, impulse buying represents a way of coping with an emotional craving that is not otherwise being satisfied. (They need to remember Principle 6: *You can never get enough of what you don't need, because what you don't need can never satisfy you.*) For most people, however, impulse buying is merely a reflection of poor shopping habits and a lack of self-discipline.

Such habits can often be overcome simply by making out a shopping list and sticking to it, by not carrying credit cards or checkbooks with you, and by agreeing to establish built-in time delays proportional to the size of the purchase—for example, waiting 24 to 48 hours before making large purchases. Ask yourself, "Do I really need this, or do I merely want it?" A quick review of consumer products reveals that more than 50 percent of the items you have the impulse to buy today didn't even exist ten years ago. Apparently there was a time when you got along without them.

Failure to Determine the True Cost of a Purchase

It's amazing how much denial and rationalization we use to convince ourselves that we can afford something we know we cannot afford. We might say, "The computer only costs $1,200, and it will pay for itself with what it saves us on balancing the checkbook." That's quite an expensive calculator! And the $1,200 price tag is not even the *true cost* of the computer. In addition to taxes and interest charges, add the costs of a color monitor, printer, paper, printer ribbon, software, computer desk, floppy disks, disk storage boxes, and so on, ad infinitum. It could take a lifetime before the money saved from balancing your checkbook makes up for the cost of the computer.

This example may be an exaggeration—no one buys a computer just to balance the checkbook—but the principle is true. Most people can barely afford many of the things they buy, and the true cost of the items often turns out to be far greater than the initial purchase price. The *true cost* includes the initial cost, hidden costs, indirect costs, and relationship costs. When these costs are taken into account, they can easily move you from the realm of "*just barely*" to "*just buried.*"

Hidden and Indirect Costs

After making an initial purchase, you must often buy additional things to make your purchase work better. It is imperative that you include the cost of these add-ons with the original purchase price. For instance, if you buy a stereo, you soon discover that to get full fidelity you need to add a compact disc player. Then you need compact discs. By then, the speakers are no longer adequate, and so on. A large part of your indebtedness may be a result of the *hidden* costs of buying something.

Similarly, *indirect* costs such as operating, maintaining, and repairing an item must be taken into account as part of the true cost. One definition of a boat is a hole in the water into which you pour money. Swimming pools, from a financial point of view, have also been known to be bottomless.

Ask yourself the following questions to determine the hidden and indirect costs of a contemplated purchase:

1. When purchasing a car, do you need extras like undercoating, pinstriping, and extended warranties? These items, tacked on in what is called "back-end loading," can cost you.

2. What items are included in the closing costs when you purchase a home? Is the buyer or the seller going to pay for certain items such as repairs, taxes, appraisals, and inspections?

3. What accessories are needed for the item to operate as intended? Does it require battery packs, transmitters, additional games, software, printers, saddles, trailers?

4. What are the legal costs, such as registration, insurance, license fees, and property taxes?

5. What are the operational costs, such as fuel consumption, tire replacement, food requirements (for example, hay or oats), electricity, updating, depreciation?

6. What are the maintenance and repair costs, such as oil changes, antifreeze, air conditioning, veterinarian fees, storage facilities?

7. What are the costs of holiday extras: long distance calls, cards, stamps, travel, special foods, decorations, and additional electricity?

Relationship Costs

More subtle, but equally important to consider when determining the true cost of a purchase, are *emotional* and *time* costs: How might the new purchase affect relationships? For example, you may have gotten a real bargain, from a dollar-cost standpoint, on a "four wheeler" (all-terrain vehicle). Yet, because a second income is required to pay for it, the time costs may interfere with your ability to take the vehicle out in the country and enjoy it. You may also have less time to spend with loved ones. You may be more tired. Feelings of resentment may develop. These emotional costs are high.

Resentment is especially likely when you make a purchase despite the protests of your spouse, or when he or she feels that the purchase is more important than the relationship. Statements such as these may be warning signs: "Maybe if I wore a hood ornament, you'd spend as much time with me as you do with that car." "Since I can't sit on your white satin couch, just where am I supposed to sit?" Relationships with *things* might appear safer than relationships with *people*, but they cannot be as satisfying. Remember Principle 3: *Nothing (no thing) is worth risking the relationship.*

Failure to Analyze the Cost Per Use

You want to finish off a section of your basement. To frame the walls you need to attach the two-by-fours to the basement floor. To accomplish this, you buy a nail gun that fires nails through wood into concrete. The gun costs almost $400, and you use it on this *one* project. The cost per use is $400. If you use the gun on two projects, the cost per use drops to $200 ($400 divided by 2). But you could *rent* the gun for $20 per use.

Cost-per-use consideration should be given to just about everything you have the urge to buy, including mountain cabins, boats, four-wheel-drive vehicles, cellular phones, airplanes, scuba gear, high-powered night vision scopes, and so on. For example, you may be considering a $25,000 mountain cabin. The cabin is snowed in much of the year, and the roads are too muddy to use during the spring. Primary use is limited to summer and fall.

Interest charges, property taxes, organizational dues, and maintenance and repair can easily bring the *true cost* to between $50,000 and $75,000 per year, not including furnishings. If your family went to the cabin one weekend each month during those two seasons, the cabin would be used six times per year. The mortgage payments would run about $375 per month ($25,000 at 13 percent for 10 years). Add another $125 per month in taxes, dues, and maintenance costs, and you have a monthly payment of $500 per month or $6,000 per year. This means that the six visits to the cabin would cost $1,000 each, not including travel expenditures. You could rent a fantastic cabin for $100 per night or $200 per weekend—a fraction of the cost of purchasing your own cabin.

Cost-per-use calculations can let you determine if there are more economical ways to fulfill your needs, such as renting, borrowing, or sharing. Sharing can be especially effective between cooperative neighbors and extended family members. *One* rototiller could be used for five yards, for example, or *one* snowblower for three driveways.

Lack of Adequate Insurance Coverage

Lack of adequate insurance can put people in financial straits almost as fast as unemployment. Some of the most neglected forms of coverage are major medical, disability, liability, and life. In many cases, the car and house are adequately covered, but the people in them are not.

Insurance protects us from rare but potentially very costly events. The rarity of these events leads many to believe that they do not need insurance, so they try to get by without it, leaving themselves open to financial disaster. It's important to review medical, life, and property insurance policies on a yearly basis or whenever there is a change in the size or composition of the family. (For more on insurance needs, see chapter 7.)

Credit Abuse

Many people don't realize until it's too late that they're getting into serious financial difficulties. Because of the behaviors already discussed, they live beyond their means, abuse credit, and one day find themselves staggering under a heavy debt load. Following are danger signs that warn of impending financial disaster, as well as suggestions for effective use of credit.

You don't think of credit as debt. More than two-thirds of all families use some type of credit card, and nearly 50 percent of them pay off their account balance each billing period.[3] Those who don't pay off the balance on a monthly basis see credit cards not as a short-term substitute for cash but rather as a convenient means of taking out a loan. Many don't realize that when they make statements such as "I'll just put it on the Visa" or "Let's just charge it," they are in reality saying, "Let's go into debt for it." Stop thinking of your credit card's limit as a line of credit, and begin thinking of lines of credit as lines of debt.

You have to borrow to make payments to creditors. Picture yourself on a boat in the middle of the ocean. The boat has ten holes in the bottom and you have only nine corks. No matter how you move the corks around, endlessly pulling a cork out of one hole in order to use it to plug another, your boat will eventually sink. The same principle applies to using cash advances from one credit card to make payments on another, or taking out a new loan on the car to make mortgage payments. To avoid getting into this kind of financial bind, determine affordable payment amounts *before* you acquire a debt.

You have more than seven consumer-credit loans. You are living beyond your means and expecting others to support your lifestyle (see *Trying to Move Too Far, Too Fast,* this chapter). As each creditor says, "That is all I care to contribute," you must find someone else who is willing to bankroll your excesses. To avoid such pretentious living, limit credit use to major purchases only, involving no more than two or three creditors altogether.

You use more than 20 percent of your take-home pay to make credit payments. Excluding your mortgage payment, installment debt should not exceed 20 percent of what you take home after taxes. For a person taking home $1,500, monthly payments for debt should total no more than $300. In many cases, car payments alone meet or exceed this limit, but for some reason car payments are often thought of separately from other consumer debt items, such as furniture, household appliances, and clothes. Be sure to include everything but the mortgage when you total up your credit payments.

All of your family's second-earner income goes to pay debts. Dual-income families in the lower-income group lose about 46 percent of their increase to job-related expenses, while those in the middle-income group lose about 56 percent, and those in the upper-income group lose about 68 percent. Job-related expenses include tax, Social Security, health care deductions, life insurance premiums, contributions to retirement funds, union or professional dues, extra clothing, uniforms and cleaning, meals out, transportation costs, and child care expenses. What's left will usually pay just some of the bills.

(Not surprisingly, even with these additional expenses, the dual-income family has some advantage over the single-income family. The size of this advantage varies with the wage earners' income group. Dual-income families in the lower-income group usually realize a 70 percent increase in income over a single-income family. Those in the middle-income group realize a 38 percent increase, while high-income families realize only a 16 percent increase.)

Because a second income yields less in actual usable funds than you may have thought, the amount you can use for debt repayment may not be large enough. It is important that you realize this before taking on a second income in order to pay off debt.

You use credit cards impulsively. A good rule of thumb is that the item purchased should last longer than the payments. Paying for vacations and meals usually lasts longer than the trip or dinner. Imagine reading a restaurant's menu to a loan officer and saying, "The New York steak looks good to me, but then the fresh lobster is always superb. What do you think? Can we qualify for a loan that's big enough to get both?" At first this may seem a little ridiculous, but when you charge your dinner rather than pay cash for it, you are in effect asking the bank if you can borrow money to pay for your meal. As a mark of your dedication to using sound financial principles, agree to use credit cards only for preplanned purchases of durable goods, or in emergencies.

You don't pay accounts on time. From time to time, even large businesses experience a cash flow problem when the costs of purchases and overhead exceed the amount of money coming in. If this condition is only temporary, the businesses can ask their creditors for some additional time to fulfill their financial obligations. But if this condition continues over a long period of time, the businesses go bankrupt. They spend faster than they earn; eventually this practice catches up with them. The same rule is true for individuals.

Few things in life cause more stress than getting behind on bills. Past-due notices and calls from collection agencies can create financial, emotional, and social stress that can be devastating. To avoid this stress, create a reserve account or subtract credit card purchases just as you would checks (see chapter 7).

You make only minimum credit payments each month. Many bank card repayment plans are set up so the cardholder must pay only 1/36 of the principal due, plus interest. In effect, the bank is saying, "We don't want you to pay off your outstanding balance too quickly, because we want to continue making an outrageous profit." The cardholder may pay up to 21 percent interest, in addition to an annual fee equivalent to another 1–3 percent. This, plus the 3 percent that the retailer pays to the bank, can result in a hefty 27 percent return for the bank. That obviously beats the interest rates that could be earned on a home loan. To avoid paying high interest rates, accelerate payoff schedules by adding as much extra principal as possible to each payment (see chapter 6).

Your debt repayment schedules are longer than one year. Excluding your home mortgage, student loans, and most car loans, the duration of a loan should not exceed *one year*. Ideally, this should apply to car loans as well, but with the average cost of a new car approaching $20,000, it's unrealistic to expect to pay off a car in one year. In the "good old days," car manufacturers operated on a three-year style-change cycle, and car loans were made for one- or two-year periods. But the price of cars has risen faster than has the ability of most people to pay for them. To compensate for this discrepancy, car loans are now offered for five-, six-, and even seven-year periods. The car dealer is basically saying, "On your income, you couldn't possibly make the payments necessary to pay the car off in one year" (translated: "You can't afford it—period"). So the amount of the monthly payments has been reduced, allowing you to make more payments over a longer period of time.

Consider three consequences of these financial manipulations:

1. The buyer can end up with interest charges amounting to almost as much as the purchase price of the car.

2. It is not until three or four years into the loan that the value of the car begins to exceed the amount still owed on the loan. (Of course, a large down payment can decrease the size and duration of the loan, as well as the amount of interest paid.)

3. The longer the term, the harder it is to count on financial stability. How stable can you expect your financial world to be during the next five to seven years? As you look back over the past five years, do you find that life has gone the way you expected, or did you have a few surprises?

If you would like to buy a $5,000 car, have only about $200 per month available for payments, and want to pay the car off in one year, try the following: Make a $210 payment to your *savings account* each month for one year. At the end of the year, you'll have approximately $2,600 (including 3–4 percent interest). Put the $2,600 down on the car and finance the remaining $2,400 for twelve months at $211 per month ($2,345 at 10 percent = $2,532 divided by 12).

If you were to finance the whole $5,000, you could make monthly payments of $231 for 24 months (at 10 percent per year). But by saving for a year, you earned interest instead of paying it, and you were in debt for only one year instead of two. Thus, your car is paid for in the same two-year period and your net interest costs dropped from $544 to about $132.

Whenever possible, calculate and commit to only a one-year payoff schedule—except for most car and education loans.

You are considering consolidating loans. Consolidation loans are helpful only if you have corrected the behavior that led to the problem in the first place. Otherwise it will be just a matter of time before the problem resurfaces and drives you even deeper into debt. You may find that you are better off using the fold-down method described in chapter 6 to decrease your debt load and amount of your monthly payments.

Addictive Behavior and Finances

Sixty-six percent of people in the United States over 15 years of age drink alcoholic beverages on occasion. Fifty-eight percent drink at least once a month, and 10 percent drink at least one ounce of alcohol per day (the equivalent of two mixed drinks, two glasses of wine, or two cans of beer). One in ten users becomes an alcoholic.[4]

All addictive behaviors are costly, in both financial and human terms. The financial and personal costs of cocaine addiction are well known, as are the costs of becoming addicted to other illegal drugs, prescription drugs, alcohol, and tobacco. The financial devastation of an addiction stems not only from the exorbitant costs of some of these substances but also from the personal deception created to justify such habits. If the substance abuse involves an illegal drug, trying to create a family budget is useless because *all* of the family resources will eventually be devoted to obtaining more of the drug.

If legal drugs (alcohol, tobacco, or prescription drugs) are involved, the cost of the substance should be included in the budget. In this way, those directly and indirectly involved will realize exactly how much money is being spent on addictive substances. For example, two or three cans of beer per day add up to two or three six-packs a week. At $5 or $6 a six-pack, this can add up to between $40 and $80 per month.

In many instances, users deny how expensive their habit has become. With the costs of the addictions being recorded as part of the family budget, however, denial becomes impossible. In addition, the accumulated costs of the habitual consumption can be assessed from a relative value standpoint (see chapter 1). For instance, the previously noted beer consumption costs could reach $1,000 per year. Is there some other way you would have preferred to spend that $1,000? Is your money, as Principle 4 admonishes, going to what you value?

Gambling and compulsive buying are also addictive pathological behaviors that can bring financial ruin and personal heartache, both to those directly involved and to their loved ones. In most cases, it is necessary to seek professional help to overcome addictive or compulsive behaviors.

Behaviors Associated with Effective Financial Management

If you really want to get out of debt and stay out of debt, then you must drop old habits and establish new ones. Effective financial management includes the following behaviors:

1. Make purchases appropriate to your income.

2. Set limits on your needs and wants; decide what would be "enough" house, car, income, and so on.

3. Take advantage of educational resources—libraries, schools, and seminars—to learn budgeting and management skills.

4. Agree to build in time delays proportional to the size of the purchase you are considering.

5. Calculate hidden and indirect costs along with the original purchase price.

6. Consider whether renting, borrowing, or sharing might be more economical than buying.

7. Periodically review medical, life, and property insurance policies to make sure they are adequate in light of your present circumstances.

8. Think of lines of credit as lines of debt, and use them only for emergencies and planned purchases of durable goods.

9. Seek professional help regarding addictive or compulsive behaviors.

NOTES

1. Krueger, 1986.

2. Aristotle, 1952, 452.

3. Canner and Cyrnak, 1985.

4. U.S. Department of Health and Human Services, 1990.

CHAPTER **6**

DEBT MANAGEMENT

Some people equate the process of managing debt with juggling in a dark room: they never know what's going to come down on them next. Some seem to accept the stress associated with managing debt as a normal part of consumer life in the twenty-first century. Others avoid debt as they would the plague; debt to them is a destructive force capable of abolishing the American promise of life, liberty, and the pursuit of happiness. To appreciate one way of looking at debt, it may prove helpful to take a brief look at one aspect of our nation's history.

Debt as Indentured Servitude

When America was first being settled, many who wished to come to the new land didn't have enough money to pay for passage. Yet their desire to come to America was so great that they offered to work off the cost of their passage by becoming someone's servant if that person paid their way. These immigrants were called *indentured servants*. Such a servant might be defined as anyone who contracted to pay off a debt by working for the creditor for a specified period of time.

A number of similarities can be found between indentured servants and borrowers in today's financial world. Let's say you want to buy a car. The price of the car is about $13,500, and the bank agrees to finance the loan at 13 percent interest for five years. You will make 60 monthly payments of about $307 each, paying a total of $18,400 for the car. You will have to earn around $500 per month in order to clear enough money (after taxes are deducted) to make the $307 payments.

Assume your gross income (before deductions) is about $2,000 per month. So the $500 you need to make the car payment represents 25 percent of your monthly salary. In essence, this means *you have agreed to work one week (25 percent of your time) out of every month for the next five years for the bank so you can have the new car.* You have just become an indentured servant for the next five years. This is what indebtedness really means.

If you don't like the idea of being an indentured servant, you will want to get your debts under control. The first step is to stop going further into debt. Then you must decide whether to increase your income or decrease your expenses to get out of debt. Based on this decision, you must then develop a plan to start getting out of debt. Throughout the process, you can learn to cope with the stress that accompanies a financial crisis.

Stop Going Further into Debt

Remember Principle 2? *If you continue doing what you have been doing, you will continue getting what you have been getting.* This is especially true for chronic indebtedness.

Imagine two people trying to survive in a boat in the middle of the ocean. One of them asks the other, "What are you doing?" and is told, "I'm plugging the holes in the bottom of the boat. What are you doing?" The first person answers, "I'm poking holes in the bottom of the boat." This analogy clearly describes what happens when one person tries to get out of debt while a partner continues to increase the debt. To become free of debt, *everyone* involved must stop doing whatever it is that has been getting them into debt.

It stands to reason that if you are an alcoholic and wish to recover, you must stop drinking. If you are a compulsive gambler, you must stop betting. And if you are chronically in debt, you must stop borrowing. Otherwise, things will go on as before. If you truly want to get out of debt, determine to get out now: *no more charging, no more borrowing, and no more buying until you have enough money to pay for the purchase.*

Delay Buying

One of the prime causes of debt is impatience: "I want it and I want it NOW!" And for that we are willing to pay enormous interest charges. *Impatience can be a very expensive emotion.* In many cases, with the passage of time and a look at the consequences, "I want it" can become "I *thought* I wanted it." For this reason, you should include delays as part of the process of deciding to make a major purchase. You may want to use this principle: "The larger the purchase, the longer the delay." In other words, if something is going to cost $500, then agree to wait at least 24 hours before making the purchase. If the cost is over $1,000, wait 36 hours; over $5,000, wait 48 hours, and so on. You may be surprised at how many times you'll be glad you decided to wait and didn't make the purchase after all—and didn't apply for yet another loan.

Stop Qualifying for Loans You Don't Really Qualify For

When you take out a loan, you are usually asked to fill out a balance sheet, or statement of financial status, that lists your current assets and liabilities. You are asked to disclose your current income and to list your current debts, such as credit cards and car loans. After you have completed your loan application, the bank runs a credit check and takes a look at your income-to-debt ratio to decide whether you qualify for (i.e., can handle the expenses of) the new loan.

However, as the old saying goes, "The only time a bank is willing to give you a loan is when you don't need one." Because of this, when filling out loan applications, some people try to make themselves appear better off than they actually are. A real problem arises when they exaggerate their income, "forget" to list certain expenses, and then just barely qualify for the loan. Suppose a couple's take-home pay is about $2,000 per month. Twenty percent of that amount, or $400 per month, is the maximum amount most banks would allow the couple to commit to consumer debt. Their credit card, car loan, and furniture payments add up to $350, and they are applying for a new loan for a hot tub. The loan officer recognizes that the hot tub loan would put them slightly above the credit-limit guideline. But if they have been good customers, she may reluctantly approve their loan.

After they sign the papers, the husband nudges his wife and whispers, "It's a good thing we didn't list our $200 boat payment on the application. If we had, we probably wouldn't have qualified for the loan." He's absolutely right—they wouldn't have received the new loan if they had included anything near $200 more per month on their list of liabilities.

Many people who make "boat" payments neglect to list them on their loan applications. The "boat" can be any number of monthly financial obligations—from charitable contributions, to nursing home expenses, to private loans from friends or relatives who helped them out when they were in a bind.

The point is, you may assume some financial obligations without contracts or official records. However, these agreements can become as much a part of your financial indebtedness as a loan from a bank. If you don't list these informal obligations on loan applications, you may "qualify" for a loan you really can't afford. Even worse, as pointed out in chapter 5, actual loan payments probably represent only a fraction of what your new toy will eventually cost you each month. As a consequence, you will find yourself sinking deeper and deeper into debt, and you may end up needing to earn even more money in order to meet your financial obligations.

Increase Your Income or Decrease Your Expenses

One of the overriding truths of debt management is that to get out of debt, you must either *increase your income* or *decrease your expenses.* Most of those who find themselves buried in debt tend to favor increasing their income over decreasing their expenses. Usually, though, decreasing expenses is far more effective.

To illustrate the difference between these two debt-management approaches, look again at the situation in which you had to earn $500 to clear a car payment of approximately $300. Continuing this line of reasoning, you would have to earn $1,000 to make $600 worth of payments. But decreasing your debt load by $600 per month (perhaps by selling a car, the boat, the hot tub, or one of the horses) would have the same effect as increasing your income by $1,000 per month. That would be almost the same as getting a $12,000-a-year raise!

The way one family handled their debt problems illustrates beautifully the principle of decreasing expenses. The father taught school and the mother tended neighborhood children. One of the couple's two sons decided at the last minute to go away to college rather than join the military as planned, even though he hadn't saved for college. The parents supported his decision but knew that meeting tuition and housing expenses would be difficult. With food, books, and a few unexpected expenditures, the family's financial burden soon became unmanageable.

The son found a part-time job and the father tried working evenings at a convenience store to increase his income. However, the stress from extra work hours and constant worry began to take its toll on his health. As an alternative, the parents decided to sell one of their cars. The car payment was $300 per month, insurance was almost $100 per month, and monthly gasoline bills were over $50. In addition, the cost of registration, licensing, and maintenance easily amounted to $50 per month. Selling the car saved the family about $500 per month—more than what they needed to help out their son. From then on, even after their son returned home for summer break, the father carpooled with other teachers at his school.

This example illustrates how one couple learned to manage their debt as well as how to cope effectively with unexpected expenses. Often the best way out of a financial hole is to decrease expenses rather than increase income. Remember that your attempts to "earn" your way out of debt could put you in a higher tax bracket, which, because of taxes, could leave you with an even smaller percentage of your extra income available for debt payments.

Start Getting Out of Debt

The basic idea behind getting out of debt is to pay off as much as possible, as fast as possible, without acquiring any additional debt. Two helpful techniques can make getting out of debt much more realistic: *accelerated repayment* and *the fold-down plan.*

Accelerated Repayment

Accelerated repayment means paying off the principal quickly in order to reduce interest charges. In a new long-term loan, most of the money included in the payment goes toward interest charges, and only a small amount goes toward paying off the principal. But *all* of the extra money added to a regular payment goes toward paying off the principal, thus accelerating the repayment of the loan and reducing interest charges. The accelerated repayment method can be applied to almost any loan.

Table 6.1 illustrates this concept with a mortgage of $100,000. It shows that by adding an extra $25 to the mortgage payment each month, you reduce the term to maturity from 30 years to 25 years and 10 months and the interest paid over the life of the loan by about $36,000. By paying an extra $100 per month toward the principal, you reduce the term to maturity to 19 years and 3 months and the interest by about $90,000. If you take out the mortgage for a 15-year period, payments increase to $1,075 per month (about $197 more than for the standard 30-year mortgage), but you save $122,500 in interest compared to a 30-year mortgage.

In three of the four cases above, payments per month are higher, but the saving in total interest is much greater than the total payment increases. The high cost of interest cannot be overemphasized. Note that with the 15-year loan you end up paying nearly $200,000 for a $100,000 house. With the 30-year loan, you pay over $300,000— enough for three $100,000 houses!

TABLE 6.1—FOUR WAYS TO PAY OFF A MORTGAGE (ASSUMING A $100,000 LOAN AT A 10 PERCENT INTEREST RATE)

Payment Period	Payment Amount	Interest Paid	Interest Saved
30-year loan	$878	$216,000	0
Adding $25 per month: 25 years 10 months	$903	$180,000	$36,000
Adding $100 per month: 19 years 3 months	$978	$126,000	$90,000
15-year loan	$1,075	$93,500	$122,500

The Fold-Down Plan

The fold-down plan of debt elimination entails paying off one debt and then applying (folding down) that payment to another debt in a cumulative progression. The first step in this plan is to pay off one of your debts, perhaps by using your tax refund, reallocating money budgeted for entertainment, or riding the bus. Then apply the money from that debt toward paying off a second debt. When you have paid off the second debt, fold down the amount from the first two debts into paying off a third debt, and so on until you have paid off all your debts. During this process, monthly expenses remain constant, but debt payments progressively focus on fewer and fewer debts.

Table 6.2 gives an example of a fold-down repayment plan. The left side of the table lists creditors and the amount owed to each. To the right of the creditors are the monthly payments. In this example, $50 each month goes to Visa, $100 to MasterCard, $25 to Sears, and so on. A total of $1,075 per month is distributed in loan payments.

TABLE 6.2—FOLD-DOWN REPAYMENT PLAN

CREDITORS	MONTHLY PAYMENTS								
	Jan.	Feb.	Mar.	Apr.	May	June	July	Aug.	Sept.
Visa $50.00	50	paid							
MasterCard $250.00	100	150	paid	(Interest payments saved)					
Sears $225.00	25	25	175	paid					
Furniture $850.00	100	100	100	275	275	paid			
Car loan $2,650	300	300	300	300	300	575	575	paid	
Second mortgage $5,650	500	500	500	500	500	500	500	1,075	1,075
Total owed $9,675	1,075	1,075	1,075	1,075	1,075	1,075	1,075	1,075	1,075

After the January payments are made, the Visa bill is paid in full. However, instead of using that $50 somewhere else in February ("Now that we have our Visa card paid off, we can afford to buy the dining room set"), the amount of the Visa payment is applied to the MasterCard bill. As a result, in February a total of $150 is applied to the MasterCard bill, paying it off. All other payments remain the same for that month. In March, the $150 that had been allocated to the credit cards can now be added to the regular $25 payment to Sears, paying off that debt. Again, regular payments are made to all other creditors during March. In April, the extra $175 now available can be added to the $100 furniture payments. After only two months of $275 payments on the furniture, it is paid off. This process continues until the entire $1,075 is being applied to the second mortgage.

In this example, all debts have been repaid after eight months. The amount of time it will take you to pay off your debts varies with your total indebtedness and how much extra money you can use to begin a fold-down program. (Remember, *all* of what you pay over and above your regular monthly payment goes toward paying off principal.) Extra money might come from income tax returns, garage sales, brown-bag lunches, fewer long-distance phone calls, less golf, or lower utility bills.

By using the fold-down method, you save a great deal in interest charges (the sooner you pay off a debt, the sooner you stop paying interest on that debt). To be successful with this method, however, *you must curtail all nonessential consumption.* Fight the tendency to pay off one thing and then turn around and buy something else. Otherwise, you will remain in debt.

The Fold-Up Plan

After you pay off your last debt, you would be wise to continue making payments as if you were following the original payment schedule. Now, however, put the payments into your savings account, where they will *earn* you interest rather than cost you interest. By using the monthly payment amount from Table 6.2 ($1,075), you would have over $6,500 in the bank (including some earned interest) within six months. The family in this example went from being almost $10,000 in debt to having more than $6,500 in the bank in just 14 months. They rose from the bewildering stress of financial crisis to financial solvency and peace of mind.

Financial Crises and Stress

Medical doctors and financial planners complain that many of those who need their professional help seldom contact them until their problems have become all but insurmountable. When people finally do seek professional help, they expect the professional to "make things right again," regardless of the severity of their condition. In most cases, it is much easier to prevent a crisis than to cure one. But some financial crises cannot be avoided, no matter what you do.

The word *crisis* is derived from the Greek word *krisis,* which means decision. A financial crisis is a situation in which you are obliged to make a financial decision. Financial crises often occur because of death, divorce, unemployment, major illness, or overwhelming consumer debt. Whatever the cause, an inevitable by-product of a financial crisis is *stress.*

Resolving Financial Crisis

One of the most distressing emotions experienced in a crisis is a feeling of helplessness. During the initial stages of a crisis, most of us feel both helpless and hopeless. We believe there is nothing we can do to change the situation. To counter these feelings, we must—at the very beginning of a financial crisis—implement a plan to cope with the possible consequences. The following recommendations will help you develop and implement such a plan.[1]

1. Reframe the situation. Since you cannot change what has happened in the real world (stock market fluctuations, swings in the real estate markets, changes in employment, etc.), the best alternative is to reframe or change your perception of those events, as discussed in chapter 4. Reframing is the process of reinterpreting the meaning or significance of an event; it means seeing things from a different perspective. For example, you might realize that a loss in the value of your stock will have a major financial impact only if you sell your stock. Otherwise, your loss is only on paper; and if you hold on to the stock until it regains its value, you will not experience any real financial loss.

2. Avoid procrastination. Since most financial crises involve both time and money, it is essential that you not procrastinate. Immediately establish dates and deadlines by which to take certain actions. Develop contingency plans in the event your first plan of action is blocked. Establish *priorities* wherein you deal first with the most pressing tasks (legal action about to be taken or foreclosure about to be filed) and the most unpleasant tasks (contacting a creditor who has been particularly insistent).

3. Distance yourself. Putting a crisis behind you as quickly as possible can be very beneficial. Try to focus on the future rather than on the past. This is easiest if you can distance yourself from the crisis—remove or reduce factors in the present that remind you of the past.

One way in which distancing can be used is illustrated in how Brian handled the pain of a second court decree regarding his divorce. Brian and Joan divorced each other after seven years of marriage. Their divorce decree stipulated that Joan was to receive custody of their two children, and Brian was to be assessed $200 per month for each child until the children reached 18 years of age. Shortly after the divorce, Joan remarried. Joan and her new husband wanted to establish their own family and raise Joan and Brian's children as their own, without the hassle of Brian's visits and of contending with two fathers. They made a verbal agreement that if Brian would not bother them about visits, they would not bother him about child support. After the agreement was made, Joan and Brian went their separate ways.

Twenty years later, Joan sued Brian for tens of thousands of dollars in unpaid child support. The court decided in Joan's favor, and Brian, who had remarried and begun to raise a second family, was faced with writing a check for hundreds of dollars each month for fifteen to twenty years. Brian was upset about the court's decision and agonized over having to be reminded of the "injustice" by writing a check each month.

To put some distance between himself and this unpleasant task, Brian deposited a lump sum in a special account that would draw a reasonable amount of interest. He instructed the bank to make an electronic transfer each month from this account to Joan's account until the money he deposited and the interest it earned had been consumed. He would then deposit another lump sum, and the process would continue.

4. Appraise the available alternatives. If your stress comes from feeling trapped, you should attempt to generate at least *three* alternative courses of action. Try to remain receptive to suggestions from others. Don't disqualify a suggestion too quickly. For example, if your financial crisis has resulted from the death of your spouse, who was the wage earner, you might ask yourself the following questions:

    A. Is employment an option?

    B. Can you make your current assets work harder for you?

1. Could some of your savings be transferred to income-producing investments?
2. Could your spouse's life insurance policy be invested to compensate for pension reduction?
3. Could assets such as the house be sold to take advantage of the one-time capital gains exemption for the elderly?
4. Would either an equity loan or a reverse annuity be an option?

C. Can you identify areas where you can cut back on expenses?

5. Take one thing at a time. Set priorities, incorporate time buffers, and concentrate on one thing at a time. Your *first* priority should be to separate the people from the problem. Make it clear to your spouse or creditors that you are meeting to attack the problem and not each other.

You and your spouse should make a list of your top three priorities. What are your greatest concerns? What are your greatest sources of stress? Consideration of your feelings about a particular factor is essential to your development of a crisis-management plan. For example, you may owe some creditors more than others, but the feelings you associate with a certain debt can be completely independent of the amount. "A hundred fifty dollars might not seem like much, considering what I owe everybody else," you may say. "But if I can't get this mechanic off my back, I'm going to end up in some kind of institution."

6. Delegate tasks and authority. Draw on the expertise of others; don't try to solve the entire crisis by yourself. Contact a credit counseling service, a lawyer who specializes in bankruptcies, or a tax expert to help you resolve your financial situation. Their experience can save you time and resources that could be better used in dealing with the stresses in your relationships.

Allow others to give you emotional support. When a factory closes, the loss of employment can be both financially and emotionally devastating to a family and a community. During these times, mutual support and a willingness to pull together can make all the difference in how effectively the crisis is met.

7. Act responsibly. Make yourself available to your creditors. Always open the mail and answer the telephone. Focus on negotiating rather than on winning. Negotiating means conferring with each other so as to arrive at a mutually beneficial settlement (see chapter 4).

8. Cooperate with creditors. When dealing with creditors, it is helpful to remember that you once looked upon them as "friends in time of need"—or at least as members of a cooperative team. Though you may have fallen on rough times, the "cooperative team" perspective is still one of the most effective tools in dealing with creditors.

In your initial contractual arrangement, you and your creditor both agreed to fulfill obligations and act honorably and responsibly. In most cases, regardless of what has transpired since the signing of the original agreement, the moral obligation to treat each other with respect still holds (see *Moral Reasoning and Relationships*, chapter 3). This attitude is essential to negotiating a mutually satisfying arrangement.

9. Select alternative means of achieving goals. The principle of *equifinality* means that you can start from different places, take different routes, and arrive at the same destination. Be imaginative and courageous. For instance, suppose you had previously planned to maintain long-term savings to finance your children's college education, but because of an unforeseen financial setback, your savings have been depleted. To still achieve your original goal of financing college education, you might (1) transfer some of your children's inheritance prior to your death, (2) establish a recyclable college fund wherein each user pays into the fund after graduating, (3) help your children apply for scholarships, grants, and loans, (4) sell some assets, (5) borrow on the cash value of your life insurance, or (6) decide not to take a particular trip or make a particular purchase. Consider other possibilities as well.

10. Adjust levels of aspiration. We often use past experiences to establish future expectations, which can lead to upwardly mobile desires. In other words, yesterday's luxuries become today's necessities. When families experience a prolonged period of prosperity, expectations of an ever-increasing ability to consume become an integral part of the family financial management process. "The more the family members feel they must have, the smaller the chance of gratifying their wants and the greater the possibility of these expectations creating financial problems," write social science researchers Hogan and Bauer.[2]

Adjusting your levels of aspiration often involves compromise or accommodation. You and others involved must be willing to settle for only part of what you had originally wanted. Sometimes, though, only the time or sequence needs to be adjusted, while the expectation remains the same. For example, you may decide to buy a new car next summer instead of this summer; or you may decide to fix up the family room first and remodel the kitchen later, instead of the other way around.

During family negotiations, it is essential that all family members express what their goals and aspirations really represent to them. Often, by adjusting levels of aspiration, family members will be able to realize at least a portion of their wants as they make wise financial decisions that benefit the family as a whole.

NOTES
1. Poduska, 1989.
2. Hogan and Bauer, 1988.

CHAPTER **7**

PLANNING FOR THE FUTURE

One of the most common complaints about family budgets is "They don't work!" Many say in discouragement, "Budgets look great on paper, but as soon as you think you're getting on top of things, an eight ball ruins everything." Eight balls—the things that sabotage budgets—are usually unexpected and often come at the worst possible time. The car battery goes dead, the washing machine breaks down, someone chips a tooth, a daughter decides to get married and wants a big wedding, a son wins the debate competition and needs money for a trip to the capital. All these are examples of eight balls, and they just keep rolling in.

Since traditional budgets are not designed to handle these unexpected events, most families try to cope by consolidating old loans, taking out new loans, or using credit cards. "Robbing Peter to pay Paul" becomes a way of life; budget allocations are juggled so much that the original categories and amounts are no longer recognizable. The budget just doesn't work.

Future events, both expected and unexpected, affect the budget. To be able to cope more effectively with inevitable "eight balls," you need to become more future oriented. Successful living requires careful financial planning and goal setting.

Setting Goals

Because wants usually exceed resources, we need to establish priorities and set financial goals. In most financial situations, we can't afford to satisfy all our wants. More often than not, we fail to achieve a particular goal because we had other conflicting goals that seemed, at the time, more important. We sometimes fail to meet long-range goals because funds keep getting diverted to short-range goals. Setting and reaching goals requires that we achieve one goal before tackling another.

Goals and Behavior

Goals are objectives worth working for. Budget goals may include saving for a down payment on a home, paying off a debt, buying a new car, or paying for an education. Long-range goals take more than a year to achieve; short-range goals take less than a year. In either case, you must establish goal-seeking behavior in order to reach your goals.

Actions that bring people closer to their goals—the steps needed to achieve objectives—are called *compatible* behaviors. *Incompatible* behaviors will delay, or even prevent, the reaching of goals. To reach a goal of saving $15,000 for college tuition, for example, a compatible behavior is to save $100 each month for the next 10 years. Spending that $100 on stereo equipment, computer accessories, and Visa payments would be incompatible behavior.

How Will You Achieve Your Goals?

Most goals, unless actively worked for, will not be achieved. Worksheets 7.1 and 7.2 (pages 131–132) will help you identify specific long- and short-range goals and steps you can take to achieve them. They can serve as a starting point for a family discussion.

Because many of your goals are in some way related to finances (feelings of security, buying a home, paying for college), allocating money to fund these goals is a prime consideration. Without stabilizing both your income and your spending, and establishing a dependable, consistent savings program, you will have difficulty achieving your goals.

Stabilizing Your Income

The financial ideal is for both income and spending to be as constant and steady as possible. In most cases, monthly income is regular and predictable, but for many occupations, such as those that are seasonal or dependent on commissions or successful project bids, it is not. When the size and frequency of income is unpredictable, an *income-draw system* can help stabilize income/expenditure difficulties.

An income-draw system is based on a predetermined monthly withdrawal from a particular account. First, set up two separate bank accounts. Deposit all of your income into Account A, as you receive it. Then decide how large your "salary," or monthly draw, will be. For instance, if you decide you need $2,000 a month for all your expenses, that amount would be drawn from Account A once a month on a specific date. This withdrawal becomes your "salary." The salary amount should be constant and not change from month to month. It is deposited in Account B, from which you pay all monthly financial obligations.

The amount you deposit in the first account will vary from month to month, but it should accumulate enough of a reserve to ensure continuous availability of funds in excess of the monthly "salary." This is how it works: Suppose it is January. After you've set aside the funds necessary to meet tax obligations, your January income is $2,500 and you withdraw your $2,000 salary. The reserve in Account A will be $500. February's income is $3,500. The $2,000 salary is withdrawn, leaving $2,000 in the reserve. March's income is only $1,500, but you can still withdraw your usual salary, leaving a reserve of $1,500. April's income turns out to be only $1,000; nevertheless, you are able to withdraw $2,000, leaving $500 in the reserve.

Unless you happen to have an especially good month when you start your income-draw system, you may have to take a reduced "salary" until your reserves build up. Put aside small amounts each month for several months until you accumulate enough to cover normal monthly draws. At the end of the year, if you have money left over in your Account A reserves, you can consider increasing your "salary" for the upcoming year. If you find your reserves frequently being depleted, you may consider decreasing your draw during the next year. To easily facilitate this kind of system, most banks will arrange for an automatic transfer of funds from one account to another.

The income-draw system enables you to enjoy a steady income and get off the financial yo-yo that people with irregular incomes often experience—having money to burn one month and buying food on credit the next.

Stabilizing Your Spending

Once you've stabilized your income, you're in a better position to project amounts to budget for various expenditures. To stabilize your spending, you must consider both current and future expenditures. One way to stabilize current expenses is to opt for *equal payment programs,* such as those offered with fuel, utility, and city services.

To stabilize future expenditures, learn to think of certain categories as *spent but not collected,* and create an *amortization reserve.*

Spent but Not Collected

Most budgets are set up to pay monthly bills. But what about money you owe that's not collected during the current month? You'll probably spend it on something else, and when the bill does arrive you decide to pay it with the food money. From there your budget goes out the window.

This kind of financial mistake comes from thinking that because you do not have to pay a particular bill during the current month, you are free to spend the money on something else. In reality, however, you have already spent the money—it just hasn't been collected by the creditor yet.

To illustrate, take a look at last month's long-distance telephone bill, utility bill, or credit card statement. When you make a long-distance phone call, you are running up a bill; it's just not collected at that moment. The same thing happens when you turn on the lights, heat some water, or run the air conditioner. The meter may be running now, but the bill isn't due for another month.

Think of a vacation in a nice hotel. You have fresh linen daily, you eat dinners at a fine rooftop restaurant, and you enjoy cold sodas by the pool. All you have to do is write down your room number and sign your name. No one collects any money from you until the day you check out (or even later if you use a credit card).

Now think: Was there any doubt in your mind that the room cost $120 a day, that you paid more than $60 each time you ate on the rooftop, or that the soft drinks delivered to you at poolside cost $2.50 each? Though you were *spending* the money, the hotel was not *collecting* it—until the day you checked out. The same thing happens at home. When this concept is not considered, the eight balls will keep rolling in and budgets will continue to self-destruct.

So what's the answer? How can a person who wants to develop a viable budget incorporate the idea that money is continually being spent but not collected? The answer lies in amortization.

Amortization of Expenses

Amortization means spreading payments over a period of time, as when you pay for something in installments rather than in one lump sum. This is not a recommendation to take out a loan, but rather a recommendation to *pay as you go* by making average monthly payments on bills that come due semiannually and annually.

Obviously, your income will not suddenly go up when these periodic financial obligations come due, so to have money available, you need to set aside the cost of these services and items on a regular basis. Calculating and making average monthly payments—amortizing—will keep your expenditures constant. Rather than pay a lump sum of $1,200 for property taxes in January, for example, you can amortize your annual tax assessment by depositing in a bank account $100 per month throughout the year. Similarly, you may need to deposit $28 per month to pay for the annual car registration fee, and $12 per month to cover costs of professional dues when membership renewal comes around. When you follow this principle, things like taxes, car registration, and dues are no longer eight balls but normal *budgeted* obligations instead.

If you're paid weekly or twice a month, amortizing your monthly bills can also be beneficial. Most people pay each monthly bill from the paycheck that arrives nearest to the bill's due date. This process usually results in "feast or famine." Suppose, for example, you pay rent out of the first $700 check of the month and the car payment out of the second. Rent is $500, so you have only $200 left to live on during the first two weeks of the month. But the car payment is only $200, which leaves $500 to live on the second two weeks of the month. To smooth out this roller-coaster existence, amortize the bills by taking $250 for rent and $100 for the car payment out of *each* paycheck. In this way, you will have the same amount of money ($350) to live on during both two-week periods of the month.

Most people have a pretty good idea of their monthly income, but monthly expenditures are less predictable. One month might have few expenditures; the next month might have many. Most budgets are unable to adapt to such fluctuations and soon become inoperative. The purpose of amortization is to make the outgo as steady and predictable as the income.

You must account for four categories of expenditures when amortizing: *scheduled fixed, scheduled variable, unscheduled variable,* and *savings/investments.* On Worksheet 7.3, Monthly Expense Amortization (page 133), record your expenses in each of these categories. Then divide the total amount by 12 so that the necessary funds can be set aside on a monthly basis until the time comes to make the actual payments.

Scheduled fixed expenses are usually either legal agreements such as car insurance and registration, life insurance, and property taxes, or are large annual or semiannual expenses such as tuition and school fees. All debts that come due according to a predetermined schedule and for a fixed amount fall into this category.

Even though we know these things are coming and how much they will cost, we often fail to plan for them. As a result, when we can least afford it, we get a nasty surprise in the mail. To incorporate fixed obligations into a budget, you must remember that the car registration does not cost $84 for the month it comes due; it costs $7 every month of the year, *collected once a year.* Each month you should include $7 for car registration in your budget, and that money should be set aside as if it were already spent (because it is). Then, when the $84 comes due, the money is sitting in a bank account ready to be used, and your budget remains intact. All scheduled fixed expenditures should be divided into monthly payments with this amount set aside.

On Worksheet 7.3, record the date and dollar amounts of your scheduled fixed expenses. Add each row and enter the total at the end of the row. Add these totals to obtain the *scheduled fixed subtotal.*

Scheduled variable expenses are those that come due on a predetermined schedule but for variable amounts. Examples are birthdays, anniversaries, Christmas, and family vacations. We know exactly when these events will occur, but the amount we spend on them is somewhat flexible. Costs of these special occasions are often far more than anticipated, as mentioned in chapter 5. For instance, the cost of a birthday is not always just the cost of a gift; it may also include the cost of invitations, food, party decorations, wrapping paper, and long-distance phone calls. The cost of Easter could include new clothes and Easter baskets for each child. If, on Mother's Day, a husband spends $20 to $30 per mother, he could end up spending at least $60 if he includes his mother, his mother-in-law, and his wife. If you make no plans for these events and make no payment toward them each month, you could end up using your credit cards excessively. Of course, it's up to you just how much you decide is an appropriate amount to spend per year on these events, but it helps to determine the amounts so they can be amortized over the entire year.

Once you have decided on amounts for each occasion, record them in the appropriate spaces on Worksheet 7.3. Enter the totals of these amounts at the end of each row. Then add up these totals to obtain the *scheduled variable subtotal.*

Unscheduled variable expenses are costs of events that may or may not happen during the year. Chances are, though, some of them will happen. These are sometimes unhappy events, such as unemployment, a death in the family, a car accident, or a prolonged illness. Or they may be happy events like weddings or births.

Emergency funds and insurance are ways to manage these expenses. Use Worksheet 7.4, Emergency Fund Estimate (page 134), to calculate your *unscheduled variable subtotal.* Then enter this subtotal on Worksheet 7.3. Worksheet 7.4 will help you become aware of how much money you need to be prepared for any eventuality. The *ideal* emergency fund is large enough to cover (1) the deductibles on items covered by insurance, (2) the costs of services and property not covered by insurance, and (3) minimal living expenses for three months. Enter these amounts on the worksheet and total them on line A.

On line B, enter the value of resources that could be applied toward the emergency fund, such as the cash value of your life insurance policy and any savings you have already accumulated (keeping in mind the difference between amortized expenses and savings). The total amount you still need to deposit in order to complete your emergency fund (line C) is calculated by subtracting the resources on hand from the ideal fund amount. This savings goal can then be transferred to Worksheet 7.3 as the *unscheduled variable subtotal*.

Savings and investments is the final category to consider for amortization—and it is a vital one. Because of its importance, many people include savings in their scheduled fixed category. This reminds them to make a "payment" to savings on a regular basis in the same way that they pay their debts. In this way, goals become not just feasible but probable. For most people, stopping the foreclosure, getting out of debt, and having enough food on the table are not enough. They want a financial management plan that goes beyond keeping them alive; they want a plan that helps give meaning to life.

"Meaningfulness" plays a vital role in goal setting (see Personal Values, page 15; and Principle 4, page 10). When you spend your time in what seems to be meaningless pursuits, you're left with the question, "What difference does it make?" For instance, people without meaningful goals might think to themselves, "What difference does it make whether I work overtime? It all seems to go for taxes anyway." Or "We used to barely make it on one salary. Now both of us are working and we're still just barely making it. No matter what we do, we never seem to get anywhere."

Savings have a way of letting you know that you are getting somewhere, that you are closer to achieving your goals, and that you are doing more than just getting by. The earlier you begin a savings program, the more you will benefit from the effects of time and interest.

Table 7.1 shows how much you need to save each month at a certain interest rate in order to accumulate a specified amount over a period of time. For example, if you wanted to save $20,000 in ten years at a 5 percent rate of interest, you would need to save $128 per month; at a 10 percent rate of interest you would need to save $96 per month. If you wanted to save $20,000 in five years at a 5 percent rate of interest you must save $293 per month; at 10 percent interest you would need to save $256 per month. If the exact amount of time or interest rate you need are not shown in the table, use either the next higher number or make an estimate based on the given numbers above and below the one you need.

TABLE 7.1—THE EFFECTS OF TIME AND INTEREST

AMOUNT NEEDED	INTEREST*	1	2	3	4	5	10	15	20
				YEARS UNTIL NEEDED					
$50,000	10%	$3,944	$1,873	$1,185	$843	$639	$241	$119	$ 65
	7%	4,010	1,935	1,244	900	694	287	156	95
	5%	4,055	1,977	1,284	939	732	320	186	121
$20,000	10%	$1,578	$749	$474	$337	$256	$96	$47	$26
	7%	1,604	774	498	360	277	115	63	38
	5%	1,622	791	514	376	293	128	74	48
$10,000	10%	$789	$375	$237	$169	$128	$48	$24	$13
	7%	802	387	249	180	139	57	31	19
	5%	811	395	257	188	146	64	37	24
$5,000	10%	$394	$187	$119	$84	$64	$24	$12	$6
	7%	401	193	124	90	69	29	16	9
	5%	405	198	128	94	73	32	19	12
$1,000	10%	$79	$37	$24	$17	$13	$5	$2	$1
	7%	80	39	25	18	14	6	3	2
	5%	81	40	26	19	15	6	4	2

*Compounded monthly

Remember that the money set aside for amortized expenses is *not* savings, for in a very real sense that money has already been spent. Savings refers to money set aside *in excess* of amortized expenses; it is *not* intended to be spent during the current year.

The amount allocated for savings and investments will vary according to the circumstances and goals of each family. Enter the yearly amount you wish to allocate for *savings* as the *savings program subtotal* on Worksheet 7.3.

To complete Worksheet 7.3, add the scheduled fixed, scheduled variable, unscheduled variable, and savings program subtotals. Then divide this total of all four categories by 12 to obtain the total amount you need to set aside each month. The total will probably shock you. But keep in mind that you are probably already paying this amount—plus interest—for these various expenses. Once your debt load has been reduced by the fold-down method (see chapter 6), these payments can go into your amortization reserves.

Keeping Track of Amortization Reserves

Keeping track of your amortization reserves is easier than you might think. The first step involves recording deposits in your checking account. Normally, when you make a deposit you add that amount to the balance as recorded in your checkbook register. For example, if your checkbook balance is $100, and you deposit $1,200, you add the two, reaching a total of $1,300 in available funds. This is the *active account* portion of your checking account.

The next step is to "transfer" money from the active account portion of your account to the *amortization reserve account* portion. The money is not really moved to any other account; it is simply recorded differently. The amount of the "transfer" is deducted from your check register just as if you were writing a check. For example, if you have $1,300 in the active account and want to put $200 into your amortization reserves, you subtract $200 from the $1,300, leaving $1,100 available in the active account. But instead of recording a check number adjacent to the $200 "withdrawal" (the amount being transferred to your reserve account), place a capital *R* in the check number space (see Figure 7.1).

CHECK #	DATE	PAYEE	AMOUNT OF PAYMENT	AMOUNT OF DEPOSIT	BALANCE 100.00
	2/28			1200.00	1200.00
					1300.00
R	2/28		200.00		-200.00
					1100.00
238	2/30	City Utilities	89.50		-89.50
					1010.50

Figure 7.1. *Recording a reserve account "withdrawal" in your check register.*

You can record the amount you transfer to your reserve account in the back of the check register or in a separate accounting system. Record the date of the reserve account "deposit," and then distribute the deposit among the various amortized categories. Arrange the categories in columns so you can easily keep a running total for each one. To record and distribute the $200 from the above example, place $30 under the taxes category, $20 under car registration, $100 under college tuition, and $50 under auto insurance.

After distributing the "deposit," add up the amounts in each amortized category to determine the total accumulated to date. For example, if you had accumulated $120 in your reserve account for taxes and just "deposited" an additional $30, your new total in the taxes column would be $150 (see Figure 7.2).

| DEPOSIT/WITHDRAWAL DATE AND AMOUNT | DATE ACCOUNTS ARE TO BE PAID | | | |
| | 4/15 | 3/25 | 9/2 | 2/28 |
	TAXES	CAR REGISTRATION	COLLEGE TUITION	AUTO INSURANCE
Balance	105.00	70.00	600.00	175.00
1/25/98 ($100)	15.00	10.00	50.00	25.00
Balance	120.00	80.00	650.00	200.00
2/28/98 ($200)	30.00	20.00	100.00	50.00
Balance	150.00	100.00	750.00	250.00

Figure 7.2. Recording a reserve account "deposit."

It is imperative that you continue to perceive these amounts as money *spent but not collected!* You should never view the money in the reserve account as available for use outside of the categories for which it has been designated. The only money available for current expenses appears in the active account portion of your check register.

When you write a check for an item covered by one of the reserve account categories, you record the check normally, but instead of subtracting the amount of the check from the active account portion of your checking account, you place an *R* in the balance column of the active account and then subtract the amount of the check from the appropriate reserve account column in the back of the checkbook (see figures 7.3 and 7.4).

DEPOSIT/WITHDRAWAL DATE AND AMOUNT	DATE ACCOUNTS ARE TO BE PAID			
	4/15	3/25	9/2	3/1
	TAXES	CAR REGISTRATION	COLLEGE TUITION	AUTO INSURANCE
Balance	105.00	70.00	600.00	175.00
1/25/91 ($100)	105.00	10.00	50.00	25.00
Balance	120.00	80.00	650.00	200.00
2/28/91 ($200)	30.00	20.00	100.00	50.00
Balance	150.00	100.00	750.00	250.00
3/1/91				**–240.00**
Balance	150.00	100.00	750.00	10.00

Figure 7.3. Recording a withdrawal from the reserve account.

CHECK #	DATE	PAYEE	AMOUNT OF PAYMENT	AMOUNT OF DEPOSIT	BALANCE 100.00
	2/28			1200.00	1200.00
					1300.00
R	2/28		200.00		-200.00
					1100.00
238	3/1	City Utilities	89.50		-89.50
					1010.50
239	**3/1**	**Auto Insurance**	**240.00**		**R**
					1010.50

Figure 7.4. Recording a check drawn on your reserve account.

Risk Management

During the course of a lifetime, we experience good things and bad things. Risk management seeks to minimize the financial impact of the bad things.

The principles of risk management focus primarily on two variables: (1) the frequency at which a loss can be expected to occur, and (2) the severity of the loss that can be expected when one does occur. Risk management usually consists of one or more of the following approaches: *risk avoidance, risk reduction, risk retention,* and *risk transfer* (see Figure 7.5).

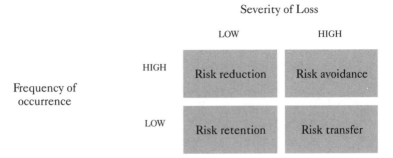

Figure 7.5. *Approaches to risk management, based on expected frequency of occurrence and severity of loss.*

Risk Avoidance

Avoiding risks is the preferred approach. An example of a risk is having an attack dog as a pet, even though you live next to a pre-school. The chances are fairly high that the dog will bite a child, and resulting liability suits could bankrupt you. To avoid this risk, you would be wise to sell or give the dog to someone else, move the dog to a kennel, or find another home.

Similarly, if you do not own a swimming pool, you avoid the risk of someone drowning, as well as a possible lawsuit. If you do not sky-dive, you avoid the risk of being killed because of a faulty parachute. If you do not walk through a high-crime district at night, you avoid the risk of being mugged, and so on.

Risk Reduction

The objective of risk reduction is to reduce both the probability and the severity of losses from events that occur with a fairly high frequency. Examples of reducing the probability of a loss include measures to protect your health, such as conducting regular safety inspections around the home and workplace, exercising, losing weight, and having annual health checkups.

Unfortunately, despite even the most diligent attempts at prevention, accidents and injury still occur. But the severity of the loss can still be reduced if risk reduction programs are in place. For example, losses can be reduced by installing fire sprinkling systems, purchasing fire extinguishers, or wearing seat belts.

Risk Retention

Some events happen with low frequency and low severity of loss. An example would be the theft of a hose from your front yard. The chances are low that it will occur, and the cost would be minimal if it did. It would be wasteful for you to pay for insurance against the loss of a $20 hose—the premiums would cost more than replacing the hose. Instead, risk retention is your best option: you "retain," or keep, the risk rather than taking any great measures to do anything about it. Many potential losses are small enough that you can just pay for them out of your own pocket. The deductible portion of your insurance policies is really a form of risk retention.

Risk Transfer

Risk transfer is the best approach to risks that have a low frequency but that can result in high financial loss. Examples of this type of risk are fires, medical emergencies, and liability suits. If these risks are retained and the event occurs, the individual or family faces financial catastrophe. Therefore, these risks should be covered by (transferred to) an insurance company. Risk transfer is the recommended approach because the cost of insurance premiums is far less than the potential cost of such a catastrophe.

Your Life Insurance Needs

The primary reason for buying life insurance is to provide financial security for your dependents. Although some individuals may use life insurance as a supplemental savings program, arguing that this provides greater assurance saving money will actually occur, most savings alternatives (certificates of deposit, employee tax-deferred matching funds, savings bonds, and so on) provide a higher rate of return.

However, there is no substitute for the financial protection life insurance provides. You may be tempted to use your life insurance for savings, but the primary reason you *need* life insurance is to guarantee financial resources for your dependents.

A couple with young children has a greater need for life insurance than does a well-established couple on the brink of retirement. Life insurance is used to help survivors meet their financial needs after the premature death of a breadwinner. Most people either underestimate or overestimate the amount of protection they need. Those who have dependents are more likely to underestimate their needs, while those who do not have dependents, and therefore do not need as much protection, tend to have too much insurance.

To avoid this paradox, review your life insurance needs on a regular basis—at least once every three years—and also whenever there is a major family change, such as a birth, wedding, death, or major home improvement.

Two of the most common techniques used to determine the amount of life insurance you need are called the *human life value approach* and the *need approach*.[1] The human life value approach projects the future income that would be lost by a person's premature death. This lump sum is then replaced by life insurance. To calculate this amount, it is necessary to (1) estimate the average annual income that would be earned through age 65, (2) deduct the amount that would be paid for all federal and state taxes, insurance premiums, and costs for self-maintenance, and (3) multiply this amount by the number of years left before retirement.

The need approach to life insurance analysis focuses on the projected cost of meeting the needs of the survivors rather than merely replacing the income that would be lost. The amount of life insurance needed is determined by adding up the estimated costs of such factors as income needs of the survivors, educational needs of the children, and medical needs of the chronically ill. Consideration should also be given to such items as the need to pay off mortgages and debts, funeral and probate expenses, and special needs such as providing for children's weddings and travel.

The money to cover all of these expenses must come from selling off assets, earnings provided by the survivors, or from life insurance proceeds. After you calculate how much your survivors can earn on their own or receive from the liquidation of your assets, you can subtract that amount from what will be needed. The rest must be covered by life insurance.

Worksheet 7.5, the Life Insurance Needs Analysis (page 135), is based on the need approach described above. It will help you understand the purpose of and need for life insurance, and it will help you decide how much insurance you need.

The first section of the worksheet, labeled "Survivor Immediate

Expense Analysis," helps you determine the assets available and the amount of money survivors would need to pay off existing debt, funeral expenses, estate taxes, and other costs. Calculate these amounts separately for each spouse. If the difference between assets and expenses is a deficit (negative), then additional life insurance is needed to correct the deficit.

In the worksheet's next section, "Survivor Income Needs Analysis," you identify sources of income and the amount of money needed to provide for your family in your absence. This does not mean you must provide a life of luxury, but there should be enough for the family to survive. Other income needed until the surviving spouse's retirement, including money for education, also falls in this category. The difference between resources and needs, if negative, represents the amount of additional life insurance needed. Add this to the amount of life insurance needed to meet immediate expenses in order to determine the total amount of additional life insurance you need.

NOTES

1. Rejda, 1982, 315–16.

WORKSHEET 7.1—WHAT ARE YOUR GOALS?

Answer the following questions as imaginatively as possible. Consider your hopes, dreams, and wishful aspirations.

1. What are five of your most important lifetime goals?

_____

_____

_____

_____

_____

2. What are five of your most important goals for the next year?

_____

_____

_____

_____

_____

3. What would be five of your most important goals if you had only six months to live?

_____

_____

_____

_____

_____

WORKSHEET 7.2—GOAL ACHIEVEMENT

Select one of the goals listed on Worksheet 7.1 and complete the following exercise. Be as specific as possible in your answers.

Goal:

_____

_____

Time within which goal is to be achieved:

_____

_____

Method of measuring progress:

_____

_____

Obstacles to be overcome:

_____

_____

What will be required:

_____

_____

Resources:

_____

_____

Action now being taken:

_____

_____

Additional action that could be taken:

_____

_____

Costs (time, energy, resources, emotional):

_____

_____

WORKSHEET 7.3—MONTHLY EXPENSE AMORTIZATION

SCHEDULED-FIXED EXPENSES	JAN	FEB	MAR	APR	MAY	JUN	JUL	AUG	SEP	OCT	NOV	DEC	TOTALS
Contributions													
Taxes													
Vehicle registration													
Educational expenses													
License renewals													
Insurance premiums													

SCHEDULED-FIXED SUBTOTALS _____

SCHEDULED-VARIABLE EXPENSES	JAN	FEB	MAR	APR	MAY	JUN	JUL	AUG	SEP	OCT	NOV	DEC	TOTALS
Birthdays													
Holidays													
Anniversaries													
Weddings													
Births													
Scouting/camping													
Home/garden maintenance													
Back to school													
Vacation													
Other													

SCHEDULED-VARIABLE SUBTOTALS _____

UNSCHEDULED-VARIABLE SUBTOTALS _____

SAVINGS PROGRAM SUBTOTALS _____

TOTAL OF ALL FOUR CATEGORIES _____

MONTHLY AMORTIZED AMOUNT (TOTAL OF ALL FOUR CATEGORIES, DIVIDED BY 12) _____

WORKSHEET 7.4—EMERGENCY FUND ESTIMATE

Amounts deductible before losses are covered by insurance
(for example, car insurance with $100 deductible)
    Automobile   _____
    Other property   _____
    Medical   _____
    Other   _____

Loss for which individual or family is responsible under co-insurance
provisions (for example, insurance may pay 80 percent and you pay
20 percent) for:
    Property   _____
    Medical   _____

Other expenses not covered by insurance   _____

Minimal family living expenses for three months
    Contractual obligations:
        Rent or mortgage payments
        Insurance premiums (on a monthly basis)   _____
    Debt payments:
        Installment credit
        Charge accounts   _____
        Outstanding bills   _____
        Other   _____
    Variable obligations:
        Food
        Utilities   _____
        Transportation   _____
        Other   _____
    Other obligations (specify)   _____

Unexpected replacement or major repair
    Automobile
    Major appliance   _____

Legal expenses

Veterinary bills

[A] TOTAL   _____

[B] Current cash value of life insurance
    and demand deposits   _____

[C] EMERGENCY FUND SAVINGS
    GOAL ([C] = [A]–[B])   _____

WORKSHEET 7.5—LIFE INSURANCE NEEDS ANALYSIS

Survivor Immediate Expense Analysis

ASSETS

	Husband	Wife
Life insurance		
Cash (savings/checking)		
Securities		
Property		
Other assets		
[A] TOTAL ASSETS		
IMMEDIATE EXPENSES AND DEBTS		
Mortgages		
Outstanding debts		
Uninsured medical expenses		
Estate taxes		
Probate		
Funeral		
Additional expenses		
[B] TOTAL IMMEDIATE EXPENSES		
[C] SURPLUS/DEFICIT = [A]–[B]		

If this figure is a deficit, it represents the amount of additional life insurance required to meet this need.

Survivor Income Needs Analysis

SOURCES OF INCOME

	Husband	Wife
Liquid assets		
Spouse earnings		
Pensions		
Social Security		
Other assets		
[D] TOTAL RESOURCES		
INCOME NEEDS		
Family income until retirement		
Education for children		
Education for spouse		
[E] TOTAL INCOME NEEDS		
[F] SURPLUS/DEFICIT = [D]–[E]		

If this figure is a deficit, it represents the amount of additional life insurance required to meet this need.

Total additional life insurance needed

[C] + [F]

CHAPTER **8**

GETTING THROUGH THE MONTH

Today's family often complains, "There always seems to be more month than money." In the "good old days," when money ran out before the end of the month, most families simply tightened their belts, stopped spending, and waited for the next payday. Those, of course, were the days when the primary medium of exchange was cash. Unfortunately, today's families usually do not stop spending when money runs out. Instead, they use credit cards as a life jacket to keep them afloat until the next payday arrives.

One of the primary reasons for using a credit card is that it enables us to obtain immediate gratification. In former times, when people wanted what another person had, they bartered. But nowadays, instead of exchanging goods, we offer our promise to pay in exchange for goods. In essence, credit cards enable us to receive what we want *prior* to working for it.

In research laboratories, rats must always press the bar *before* they are given a reward. It is contrary to the rules of motivation to first reward subjects and then ask them to labor. This would be called *reverse conditioning,* and it rarely works with rats. Apparently, it does not work that well with people either: a record 1.4 million people filed for personal bankruptcy in 1998,[1] and an untold number of people lost property to repossession.

In today's credit world, our primary concern is usually the size of the monthly payments. We then make payments on an outstanding balance for so long that we forget what we bought. We also lose sight of the actual cost of individual items, including taxes and interest charges, in the homogeneity of minimal payments. Then, as we simply add the newly acquired credit card payments (including interest) to our other monthly expenditures, next month's money runs out even sooner than last month's—and the credit cards get used even earlier in the month. Too often, this insidious progression continues until we see bankruptcy as the only way out.

Until that day of reckoning arrives, too many of us will go on believing we are living within our income. And in a sense we are—but we're not living within our budget.

Living within an Income versus Living within a Budget

Families who *live within their income* are usually able to pay all the monthly bills, but they have nothing left for amortization reserves or savings. In most of these families, the amount needed to get through the month increases at about the same rate their income increases. Often these families look back ten or fifteen years and marvel at how they used to get by on so little (even adjusting for inflation): "I used to bring home $1,500 a month and we still had a few dollars left over to play around with. Now, with both of us working, we're bringing home over $4,000 a month, and we have to charge a pizza dinner."

In contrast, families who *live within their budget* keep monthly expenditures relatively constant as income increases. They then have money for amortization reserves and savings; and the amount of money left over at the end of each month gradually increases as their income increases.

Such a surplus is possible because these families have determined what is sufficient for them to live on (see chapter 5). They have already determined what is enough house, car, and vacation. Even if they might qualify for more, they know their values and are satisfied with what they have. Should some aspect of their lives become unsatisfactory, they *decide* how much they want to spend, rather than just spending to the limit of their resources.

For example, if family members "outgrow" a house, they can either add to the existing home or buy a new one. Their decision will be based on how much they feel they *need* to spend (how much "new house" will be enough to satisfy their values), and not on how much they *could* spend (determined by the size of the loan they could qualify for with their current income). In other words, they make a budgeting choice of how much they want to spend, rather than letting the bank tell them how much they can borrow and then spending all of it.

To become a family that lives within its budget, you must learn how to cut expenses, distinguish between needs and wants, and, as discussed in chapters 5–7, incorporate into your budget the financial obligations associated with the past and the future.

Cutting Expenses

The time to cut expenses is *before* you start spending. The moment you make the decision not to spend, or at least not to spend as much as you had originally planned, you've started the process of cutting expenses. This happens, for example, when you decide to limit the purchase price of a new car to $15,000 instead of $20,000. It happens when you decide to rent an item rather than buy it, or repair rather than replace. It also begins when you borrow something from a friend or neighbor, or when you cut costs by being creative.

Sharing

Sharing can be an effective means of reducing your spending. For example, neighbors on one cul-de-sac went in together to purchase a snowblower. Friends and relatives sometimes go in on the purchase of cabins and boats. Although such arrangements may pose some drawbacks, in most cases cooperation and imagination can solve problems. Whatever the stresses of sharing, they seldom compare to the stresses of heavy indebtedness.

Plugging the Holes

The next step in cutting expenses is to "plug the holes"—the places where money seems to disappear without much to show for where it went. "Holes" are the *little things* in your spending patterns that tend to consume a *large portion* of your income.

They can appear in the form of "extras" added on to necessities: cell phones or special phone services (call waiting and call forwarding), cable TV channels, the latest and fastest home computer, or name-brand products (as opposed to the generic brand).

Nonessential Food and Drink

Consider, for example, one woman who worked for a company that made canvas awnings. The work was hard and the factory was hot, so cool drinks were a necessity. But instead of drinking water during her morning break, she bought a soda from the soft drink machine in the lunchroom, then another during her afternoon break. Each can cost 75 cents, for a total of $1.50 per day, $7.50 per week, or $30 per month. She was often tired when she got home from work, and sometimes she didn't feel like cooking. So at least twice a week she picked up fried chicken, hamburgers, or pizza. The take-home meals usually ran about $15 each, totaling $30 per week, or $120 per month. This woman was unknowingly spending more than $155 a month on pop and pizza. She had to earn about $250 a month to clear the $155 (after taxes, etc.) that went into the pop and pizza "hole."

Between-meal snacks and desserts can also be a hidden hole in the budget. Imagine saying to your spouse, "I think we should set aside $22,000 for family snacks." This suggestion may seem ridiculous and irresponsible, but you might be surprised at how fast money for snack food can add up. If your child were to have, for example, half a Popsicle in the morning (10 cents), a glass of Kool-Aid and a home-made cookie with lunch (8 cents plus 7 cents), the other half of the Popsicle in the afternoon (10 cents), and a bowl of ice cream that evening while watching TV (15 cents), the total cost for that day's snacks would be 50 cents. But what if Mom, Dad, and three or four other kids joined in? Then the daily total would come to $3, or almost $100 per month. And that translates into $1,200 per year, or almost $22,000 over an 18-year period!

These numbers are probably too conservative. Many parents who read this example may respond in mock surprise, "*One* Popsicle? *One* glass of Kool-Aid? *One* cookie? Surely you jest. That wouldn't even make *one* snack break." This example also does not include candy bars, soft drinks, gum, store-bought cookies, or the cost of repeated trips to the convenience store.

This is not to suggest that you should cut out all snacks; they can be an important part of family life. But a clear understanding of the monthly cost of treats is essential to maintaining a well-managed food budget. These examples are merely intended to help you make a conscious decision about how much you really want to spend in this category. Consider the alternative of having an extra $50 to $100 per month for bills or a vacation.

In a similar fashion, alcohol and tobacco can consume enormous portions of family income. You may not be aware of how much these items cost each month if their purchase is lumped into grocery bills or entertainment expenditures. This "hole" can be much bigger and deeper than you would expect. If a chunk of your money is going into this hole, you need to discuss the problem with your spouse with openness and honesty.

Thirty-Day Menus

Using a shopping list when you buy groceries can help stabilize your food budget, discourage impulse purchases, and enhance feelings of self-reliance.

For more efficient and less expensive grocery shopping, try a thirty-day menu. Ask family members to make a list of their favorite meals. Then, taking into account how much you wish to spend on food each month, draw from their lists to develop menus for the next thirty days. You are now able to calculate exactly how many cans of peas you will need, how many pounds of hamburger, how many potatoes, and so on.

Once you compile this shopping list, you can use it again and again. Most family members will not remember that one month ago they ate meatloaf, or that it's been four weeks since the last tuna casserole. This method allows you to equalize your food budget every month so that you can take advantage of sales on food items without worrying about overstocking your pantry. If your menu calls for eight cans of corn per month, for instance, you can take advantage of a case sale (twenty-four cans) and acquire a three months' supply of corn.

Automobile Extras

Extra car mileage can create a large hole in the budget—one you can easily reduce. The cost of driving 1,200 miles per month at fifteen to twenty miles per gallon, with gas costing $1.30 per gallon, is

$80 to $100 per month, or $160 to $200 per month if you drive two cars that much.

The first step in filling this "hole" is to monitor your driving habits for a month. Record the mileage to frequently visited locations such as malls, parks, movie theaters, supermarkets, and friends' homes. Then convert the mileage into cost-per-trip figures: Divide the miles traveled to your destinations by the miles per gallon your car gets, and multiply this answer by the price of a gallon of gasoline (miles *divided by* miles per gallon *times* cost per gallon). You can now begin thinking consciously about how much it costs to drop the kids off at Ralph's, dash down to the store, go for a drive, or visit those friends you drive 15 miles to see because you have no money for entertainment! Life offers no free trips.

After you have monitored your driving habits for a month, begin cutting out unnecessary trips. A reduction of around 15 miles a day per car could save $25 to $40 per month in a single-car family, and $50 to $80 in a two-car family. In addition, consider having children take public transportation or pay from their allowance for the "taxi service" you provide. Most children do not realize what it costs for you to take them places.

Imagine the following conversation between a parent and a child: "Mom, could you take us down to the mall so we can hang out for a while?" Mom replies, "Well, things are a little tight this month. I'll take you if you contribute a dollar toward the cost of the trip." In shocked disbelief, the child wails, "A dollar! Why should we have to pay you a dollar? It doesn't cost you anything to take us!" With a patient smile, Mom explains, "Actually, it does. Running you down to the mall would take about a dollar and a half's worth of gas. Sounds like you're getting a good deal to me!"

Try mentally adding the cost of driving to some of your destinations. For example, if you are going to a sporting event, you may spend $15 for the ticket, $5 for refreshments—and $5 for the gas to drive there. The true cost of your game isn't merely the $20 you spend on your ticket and snacks; it's $25 plus wear and tear on your car.

To further cut expenses, check into increasing the amount of the insurance deductible on your car and home. You may save quite a bit on your yearly premiums by increasing your deductible from $100 to

$250 or $500. If your car is older, you might also look into whether you really need collision coverage.

For example, if you own an older car worth $1,000 and your collision insurance deductible is $200, the most you would receive from the insurance company if the car were totaled is $800. If you're paying $300 every six months for collision insurance, in two years you will have paid more in insurance than the car is worth. In this example, canceling the collision portion of your car insurance is a more practical way to manage the risk (see chapter 7). *You should always, however, maintain the liability portion of your car insurance.*

Spending Limits

Spending limits are preestablished checkpoints designed to prevent impulsive or careless purchases. Implementing a spending limit may be as simple as limiting the amount of cash you carry with you—if you carry $10, you're likely to spend $10, but if you carry $1, you'll probably spend no more than that.

Other spending limits involve negotiating with others. You and your spouse might each agree to never make a purchase greater than an agreed-upon limit without first consulting each other. You may set a spending limit of $25, $50, $100, or even higher. By establishing spending limits, you are likely to have fewer surprises like these: "Well, what do you think of our new Saab?" or "But we needed new drapes, and they were on sale. Don't you like them?"

You can also set spending limits in certain categories. Family members may decide to spend no more than $500 for skiing in one season. They can choose to spend the $500 in one weekend or spread it out over the entire season, but when it is gone they will not use any additional funds for skiing.

Similar agreements can be made for entertainment, treats, or eating out, with set amounts allocated for a given week or month. Setting limits helps you live within your budget.

Distinguishing between Needs and Wants

A fundamental skill for living within your budget is being able to distinguish between needs and wants. A *need* is something required for survival. It provides a means to go on living, accomplishing, or contributing. A *want*, on the other hand, is something that provides greater convenience, enrichment, or pleasure. It provides motivation to continue living, accomplishing, or contributing.

Centuries ago, in A.D. 1272, St. Thomas Aquinas wrestled with the challenge of distinguishing between needs and wants and came to the conclusion that goods could be divided into two categories— *natural wealth* and *artificial wealth.* He said, "Natural wealth is that which serves man as a remedy for his natural wants, such as food, drink, clothing, conveyances, dwellings, and things of this kind; while artificial wealth is that which is not a direct help to nature, as money, but is invented by the art of man for the convenience of exchange and as a measure of things saleable."[2]

Worksheet 8.1, the Needs and Wants Exercise (page 151), will help you distinguish between your needs and wants—an important first step in creating a survival budget that will show just how little you really need to satisfy basic necessities. The first section lists alternatives that satisfy the need for transportation, including walking, biking, taking public transportation. Write any additional alternative you can think of in the blank at the end of the list. Next to the listed alternatives, record the estimated cost (monthly or annually) of each. For example, you might enter $50 in the "Walk" alternative because that is what you would spend every year on a good pair of walking shoes. Or you might enter $100 for bike repairs in the "Bike" alternative, and so on.

In the "Alternative chosen" blank, write the mode of transportation you prefer and its cost. Interestingly, you have just made a "need versus want" decision: You *need* transportation, but the way you have chosen to meet this need usually reflects what you *want.*

Compare the cost of the alternative you have chosen with the estimated costs of the other alternatives listed to arrive at the "Want Cost/Need Cost Difference" for each alternative. For example, if you choose to own a car that costs $400 a month in payments, insurance, and gasoline, subtract $50 (estimated cost for the "Walk" alternative) from $400 ("Owning one car" alternative) to produce a monthly want cost/need cost difference of $350. Record the amount in the blank. This indicates that your "want" is costing you an additional $350 per month over what it would cost you to walk. Compared to a $100-per-month public transportation cost, the one-car alternative has a monthly want cost/need cost difference of $300.

Now ask yourself: Is having a car worth an extra $300 to $350 a month in expenses? Do another cost comparison between car expenses and the cost of public transportation. The amount of money you save by using public transportation or carpooling can be substantial—perhaps hundreds or even thousands of dollars per year.

Of course, when it comes to transportation, the difference between a want and a need is determined by your circumstances. If you work at or near your home, you may be able to walk to the store or church, catch a ride with helpful neighbors, or occasionally take the bus—and not have the expense of a car at all. But if your work is farther away and not accessible to public transportation, you may have no choice but to carpool or, if that isn't feasible, drive your own car all the time. The key is to honestly determine what you need for *survival.* Once you know that, you can decide whether it's worth it to spend more for the thing you *want.* (Remember Principle 4, page 10)

Use the above procedure to evaluate shelter, food, clothing, and other needs. Table 8.1, which highlights long-distance communications, indicates the cost difference of writing letters, sending audiotapes, making long-distance phone calls, or sending e-mail. By phoning instead of writing, you pay an extra $11.36; by phoning instead of sending audiotapes, you pay an extra $10; by phoning instead of e-mailing, you pay up to $12 extra, given that certain companies provide e-mail service at no charge. (Of course, if your e-mail service comes from an internet service provider, you could be paying around $20 a month for internet access and e-mail.) Again, your circumstances help determine whether your choice is a "need" or a "want." If you simply desire to *send* communications, news, and so on, writing letters may be sufficient for you. For some, talking on the phone may fulfill an emotional need for *receiving* feedback that writing letters does not. Perhaps this need can be met in a less expensive manner. Evaluate your needs and options thoroughly, and then choose accordingly. But you must always be aware of the cost differences of choosing one alternative over another.

TABLE 8.1—THE COST DIFFERENCES OF LONG-DISTANCE COMMUNICATION ALTERNATIVES

ALTERNATIVES	FREQUENCY	ESTIMATED COST	WANT COST/NEED COST DIFFERENCE
Phone	2/month	$12.00	$ 0
Audio tapes	2/month	2.00	10.00
Letters	2/month	.64	11.36
E-mail	unlimited	0	12.00*

*Provided you receive free e-mail service and have previously invested in a home computer.

Preparing a Budget

As you have probably already guessed, an effective financial management plan can enhance the amount of satisfaction you receive from your resources. Yet only about 50 percent of families in America use some kind of budget—and only about 12 percent have one that is written down.[3] A budget is *an organized plan for meeting expenses during a given period.* It should not be seen as something that restricts your financial behavior but as something that can provide you with greater financial freedom. A budget is a road map showing you how to get where you want to go financially. Remember, your overall goal should be to spend your money on things you value, things that will last.

The budget you will develop using the principles and skills outlined in this book has a much better chance of working than your past budgets did because (1) you will include both *past* and *future* obligations to help you avoid the "eight balls" that often sabotage budgets, (2) you will consciously decide where to *cut expenses* and *plug the holes* so that your money can be applied to what you value, (3) you will take a good, hard look at what is *sufficient* to satisfy your *needs* and your *wants*, and (4) you will give consideration to the potential impact the budget might have on relationships.

To develop a workable budget, take the following five steps:

1. Evaluate how much money you *think* is coming in and from what sources, as well as how much you *think* is going out and for what purposes.

2. Compile an accurate account of what is *actually* happening financially.

3. Develop a survival budget to show how much money you would need to take care of your basic needs, rather than satisfy your wants.

4. Develop a projected budget, making a relatively accurate guess about how much money you expect to bring in and how much you expect to spend in each budget category.

5. In order to fine-tune your budget, compare your projected budget to actual income and expenditures.

Budget Categories

Following are suggested budget categories and items. The list is not exhaustive. Rather, it is designed to give you an idea of what items are typically included in each category—the same categories listed in this chapter's budget worksheets.

Income

Salary/wages: All earned income.

Other income: Includes interest, dividends, child support, welfare payments, rent subsidies, food stamps, education grants, garage sale proceeds, and inheritance.

Fixed Expenses

Taxes: Federal, state, local income taxes. (Do not include property taxes if they are included in the mortgage payment.)

Retirement programs: All contributions to retirement plans, including FICA (Social Security), company-sponsored plans, IRA, and Keogh plans.

Rent/mortgage: Rent or mortgage payments (include principal, interest, and property taxes).

Insurance premiums: Life, medical, auto, homeowner's, and any other premiums.

Vehicle license/registration: All car, boat, trailer, and airplane licensing and registration fees.

Debt repayment: Record one debt per line. The figure should reflect the total monthly payment (principal plus interest).

Other: Any other fixed expense your family has that is not included in a previous category, such as care for elderly parents or medical costs.

Variable Expenses

Food: All money spent on food, both at home and away from home (groceries, school meals, restaurant meals, meals delivered).

Utilities: Gas, electricity, water, sanitation, garbage pickup, and sewer.

Telephone: Local and long-distance service, access fees, etc.

Household operations: Repairs, cleaning supplies, gardening supplies.

Furnishings/appliances: Household furnishings, large and small appliances.

Transportation/vehicle maintenance: All bus fares, gasoline, and automobile and/or bicycle maintenance and repairs.

Apparel: New clothing and accessories, as well as laundry and dry cleaning expenses.

Personal care: Permanents, haircuts, styling, makeup, weight-loss and fitness programs.

Child care: Babysitting, day-care centers, and other forms of child care.

Education: Tuition, books, and all other costs of formal or informal education, including subscriptions to magazines and newspapers.

Recreation/entertainment: Cable TV, sporting events, movies (including video rentals), theater, club memberships, hobbies, and sporting goods.

Holidays/birthdays: All special events, such as Christmas, Easter, birthdays, graduations, anniversaries, and weddings.

Medical expenses: Any medical expenses not covered by health insurance.

Vocational dues/expenses: All expenses associated with work, including union and professional dues.

Donations: All contributions made to religious or charitable organizations.

Personal allowance: Miscellaneous expenses, including allowances for children.

Savings: Any amount put into either savings or investments and not spent during the year.

Vacation: All expenses associated with family vacations, weekend getaways, and day trips.

Other: Any other variable expenses not included in a previous category.

Your Perceived Budget

Worksheet 8.2, Your Perceived Budget (page 152), will help you and your spouse express the amounts you *think* you are earning and spending each month. Each of you should fill out a worksheet and then compare it with your spouse's worksheet. Fill in the amounts you *think* you are earning and spending monthly in each category. This exercise familiarizes you with the budget categories and sets the stage for recording your *actual* budget.

Your Actual Budget

Complete Worksheet 8.3, Your Actual Budget (page 156), after you have finished Worksheet 8.2. The same categories are included, but in this case you list the *actual* income received and the price of each item. This means digging out loan contracts, mortgages, sales receipts, W-2 forms, pay stubs, and income tax filings, and noting the exact figures. This exercise tells where your money has actually been going—and how you got into your current financial situation.

After you fill out Worksheet 8.3, compare it with Worksheet 8.2 to see how close your estimates were to the actual numbers. You will probably find some minor discrepancies between partner responses; major differences are a sign that you need more communication in those areas (see chapter 4).

This activity can be combined with a discussion among family members about where their money is really going: Is the money being spent on things you value? What changes would you like to make?

Your Survival Budget

Putting together a survival budget demonstrates how little your family actually requires to meet *minimum* needs. This budget could be used in emergencies, when income is low, or when expenses become exceptionally high (because of unexpected medical costs, for example). Worksheet 8.4, Your Survival Budget (page 158), is for recording *basic needs only*. You may be surprised at just how little your family really *needs* to survive; it is the *wants* that really cost you. Few people ever have to declare bankruptcy trying to satisfy their *needs*. It is trying to satisfy their *wants* that most often brings financial ruin.

Your Projected Budget

Worksheet 8.5, Your Projected Budget (page 159), will help you begin an accurate, effective budget. On the projected budget worksheet plan, list the amounts your family *expects* to earn and spend in each category. Try to be as accurate as possible in your estimations, but understand that even carefully considered projected budget amounts do not always reflect actual needs. After you have lived on the projected budget for a month, compare it with actual figures for that month.

Projected Budget versus Actual Budget

You may need to monitor your spending over a three-month period, making appropriate adjustments each month. Worksheet 8.6, Your Projected Budget Versus Your Actual Budget (page 161), compares the projected amounts with what you actually spent in each budget category for an entire month. This will highlight discrepancies and enable you to gradually adjust either your projected budget or your spending (or both), so that projected costs become fairly accurate approximations of the actual amounts spent. Create a file of the adjusted monthly budgets to refer to when you develop next year's monthly budgets.

You will need to develop a projected/actual comparison sheet for each month of the year. Use an income-draw system, if necessary, to even out your income, and try to keep the expenses for each month as consistent as possible by amortizing. This will help both income and expenses to remain relatively stable, regardless of fluctuations in income or the arrival of a particular holiday or special event.

NOTES

1. *World*, 7 August 1999, 15.
2. Aquinas, 1952, 616.
3. Yankelovich, Skelly and White, 1975.

WORKSHEET 8.1—NEEDS AND WANTS EXERCISE

POSSIBLE ALTERNATIVES	ESTIMATED COST	WANT/NEED COST DIFFERENCE
TRANSPORTATION		
1. Walk	_____	_____
2. Bike	_____	_____
3. Public transportation	_____	_____
4. Car pool	_____	_____
5. Owning one car	_____	_____
6. Owning two cars	_____	_____
7. _____	_____	_____
Alternative chosen	_____	
SHELTER		
1. Live with relatives	_____	_____
2. Rent apartment (one room)	_____	_____
3. Rent apartment (two room)	_____	_____
4. Buy a trailer	_____	_____
5. Buy a condominium	_____	_____
6. Buy a house	_____	_____
7. _____	_____	_____
Alternative chosen	_____	
FOOD		
1. Staples only	_____	_____
2. Home-prepared	_____	_____
3. Processed (frozen, etc.)	_____	_____
4. Fast foods	_____	_____
5. Restaurants	_____	_____
6. _____	_____	_____
Alternative chosen	_____	
CLOTHING		
1. Hand-made	_____	_____
2. Second-hand	_____	_____
3. Chain stores	_____	_____
4. Designer	_____	_____
5. _____	_____	_____
Alternative chosen	_____	
LONG-DISTANCE COMMUNICATION		
1. Write letters	_____	_____
2. Phone	_____	_____
3. Audiotapes	_____	_____
4. E-mail	_____	_____
5. _____	_____	_____
Alternative chosen	_____	

WORKSHEET 8.2—YOUR PERCEIVED BUDGET

Estimate the amounts spent monthly in each category. Those paid other than monthly are indicated by an asterisk (*). Divide annual amounts by twelve, semiannual amounts by six, and so forth, to provide the monthly equivalent.

	Income	
Husband's salary/wages	_____	
Less: Withholding taxes		
FICA taxes	_____	
Retirement programs	_____	
Subtotal of deductions	_____	
Net Income	_____	
Wife's salary/wages	_____	
Less: Withholding taxes	_____	
FICA taxes	_____	
Retirement programs	_____	
Subtotal of deductions	_____	
Net Income		_____
Other income		_____
Total Net Income		_____

	Expenses	
Fixed Expenses		
Rent/mortgage	_____	
Retirement savings	_____	
* Property taxes	_____	
* Insurance premiums	_____	
* Car license/registration	_____	
Debt repayment _____	_____	
Debt repayment _____	_____	
Debt repayment _____	_____	
Debt repayment _____	_____	
Debt repayment _____	_____	
Other _____		
Total Fixed Income		_____

Variable Expenses

    Food   _____

    Utilities   _____

    Phone   _____

    Household operations   _____

    Furnishings/equipment   _____

*   Transportation/
    vehicle maintenance   _____

    Apparel   _____

    Personal care   _____

    Child care   _____

*   Education   _____

    Recreation/entertainment   _____

*   Christmas/birthday/
    special occasions   _____

*   Medical

*   Professional dues/expenses   _____

    Donations   _____

    Personal allowances   _____

    Savings   _____

*   Vacation   _____

    Other_____   _____

                       TOTAL VARIABLE EXPENSES   _____

        TOTAL FIXED EXPENSES (from preceding page) _____

                               TOTAL EXPENSES   _____

                TOTAL INCOME LESS TOTAL EXPENSES   _____

WORKSHEET 8.2—YOUR PERCEIVED BUDGET

Estimate the amounts spent monthly in each category. Those paid other than monthly are indicated by an asterisk (*). Divide annual amounts by twelve, semiannual amounts by six, and so forth, to provide the monthly equivalent.

INCOME

Husband's salary/wages	_____	
Less: Withholding taxes		
FICA taxes	_____	
Retirement programs	_____	
Subtotal of deductions	_____	
NET INCOME	_____	
Wife's salary/wages	_____	
Less: Withholding taxes	_____	
FICA taxes	_____	
Retirement programs	_____	
Subtotal of deductions	_____	
NET INCOME		_____
Other income		_____
TOTAL NET INCOME		_____

EXPENSES

Fixed Expenses

Rent/mortgage	_____	
Retirement savings	_____	
* Property taxes	_____	
* Insurance premiums	_____	
* Car license/registration	_____	
Debt repayment _____	_____	
Debt repayment _____	_____	
Debt repayment _____	_____	
Debt repayment _____	_____	
Debt repayment _____	_____	
Other _____		

TOTAL FIXED EXPENSES _____

Variable Expenses

      Food   _____

      Utilities   _____

      Phone   _____

      Household operations   _____

      Furnishings/equipment   _____

  * Transportation/

      vehicle maintenance   _____

      Apparel   _____

      Personal care   _____

      Child care   _____

  * Education   _____

      Recreation/entertainment   _____

  * Christmas/birthday/

      special occasions   _____

  * Medical

  * Professional dues/expenses   _____

      Donations   _____

      Personal allowances   _____

      Savings   _____

  * Vacation   _____

      Other_____   _____

TOTAL VARIABLE EXPENSES   _____

TOTAL FIXED EXPENSES (from preceding page)   _____

TOTAL EXPENSES   _____

TOTAL INCOME LESS TOTAL EXPENESS   _____

WORKSHEET 8.3—YOUR ACTUAL BUDGET

Calculate the actual monthly amounts spent in each category. Those paid other than monthly are indicated by an asterisk (*). Divide annual amounts by twelve, semiannual amounts by six, and so forth, to provide the monthly equivalent. Compare the actual amounts with the perceived amounts listed previously. Note any major differences.

INCOME

Husband's salary/wages	_____	
Less: Withholding taxes		
FICA taxes	_____	
Retirement programs	_____	
Subtotal of deductions	_____	
NET INCOME	_____	
Wife's salary/wages	_____	
Less: Withholding taxes	_____	
FICA taxes	_____	
Retirement programs	_____	
Subtotal of deductions	_____	
NET INCOME		_____
Other income		_____
TOTAL NET INCOME		_____

EXPENSES

Fixed Expenses		
Rent/mortgage	_____	
Retirement savings	_____	
* Property taxes	_____	
* Insurance premiums	_____	
* Car license/registration	_____	
Debt repayment _____	_____	
Debt repayment _____	_____	
Debt repayment _____	_____	
Debt repayment _____	_____	
Debt repayment _____	_____	
Other _____		
TOTAL FIXED EXPENSES		_____

Variable Expenses

      Food   _____

      Utilities   _____

      Phone   _____

      Household operations   _____

      Furnishings/equipment   _____

  * Transportation/

      vehicle maintenance   _____

      Apparel   _____

      Personal care   _____

      Child care   _____

  * Education   _____

      Recreation/entertainment   _____

  * Christmas/birthday/

      special occasions   _____

  * Medical

  * Professional dues/expenses _____

      Donations   _____

      Personal allowances   _____

      Savings   _____

  * Vacation   _____

      Other_____   _____

                       TOTAL VARIABLE EXPENSES   _____

    TOTAL FIXED EXPENSES (from preceding page)   _____

                             TOTAL EXPENSES   _____

           TOTAL INCOME LESS TOTAL EXPENSES   _____

WORKSHEET 8.4—YOUR SURVIVAL BUDGET

Estimate the minimal monthly amounts needed for survival (needs only) in each category. Amounts paid other than monthly are indicated by an asterisk(*). Divide annual amounts by twelve, semi-annual amounts by six, and so forth, to provide the monthly equivalent.

INCOME

Husband's salary/wages	_____	
Less: Withholding taxes		
FICA taxes	_____	
Retirement programs	_____	
Subtotal of deductions	_____	
NET INCOME	_____	
Wife's salary/wages	_____	
Less: Withholding taxes	_____	
FICA taxes	_____	
Retirement programs	_____	
Subtotal of deductions	_____	
NET INCOME		_____
Other income		_____
TOTAL NET INCOME		_____

EXPENSES

Fixed Expenses		
Rent/mortgage	_____	
Retirement savings	_____	
* Property taxes	_____	
* Insurance premiums	_____	
Other _____	_____	
TOTAL FIXED EXPENSES		_____
Variable Expenses		
Food	_____	
Utilities	_____	
Household operations	_____	
* Transportation/ vehicle maintenance	_____	
Apparel	_____	
Personal care	_____	
* Medical		
Other_____	_____	
TOTAL VARIABLE EXPENSES		_____
TOTAL EXPENSES		_____

WORKSHEET 8.5—YOUR PROJECTED BUDGET

Project the monthly amounts you will spend in each category. Use the monthly amortization amounts calculated in previous worksheets where appropriate. Amounts paid other than monthly are indicated by an asterisk (*).

INCOME

Husband's salary/wages	_____	
Less: Withholding taxes		
FICA taxes	_____	
Retirement programs	_____	
Subtotal of deductions	_____	
NET INCOME	_____	
Wife's salary/wages	_____	
Less: Withholding taxes	_____	
FICA taxes	_____	
Retirement programs	_____	
Subtotal of deductions	_____	
NET INCOME		_____
Other income		_____
TOTAL NET INCOME		_____

EXPENSES

Fixed Expenses		
Rent/mortgage	_____	
Retirement savings	_____	
Scheduled fixed amortization	_____	
(taxes, premiums, etc.)		
Savings	_____	
Debt repayment _____	_____	
Debt repayment _____	_____	
Debt repayment _____	_____	
Debt repayment _____	_____	
Debt repayment _____	_____	
Other _____		
TOTAL FIXED EXPENSES		_____

Variable Expenses

Food _____

Utilities _____

Phone _____

Household operations _____

Furnishings/equipment _____

* Transportation/
vehicle maintenance _____

Apparel _____

Personal care _____

Child care _____

* Education _____

Recreation/entertainment _____

Special occasions _____

Personal Allowances _____

Scheduled variable
amortization _____

Unscheduled variable
amortization _____

Savings _____

* Vacation _____

Other_____ _____

TOTAL VARIABLE EXPENSES _____

TOTAL EXPENSES _____

WORKSHEET 8.6—YOUR PROJECTED BUDGET VERSUS YOUR ACTUAL BUDGET

Compare the monthly amounts you spent in each category with the amounts you projected at the beginning of the month. Adjust either the budget or spending for next month so the projected and actual amounts will agree.

INCOME	PROJECTED	ACTUAL	DIFFERENCE
Husband's salary/wages			
Less: Withholding taxes			
FICA taxes			
Retirement programs			
Subtotal of deductions			
NET INCOME			
Wife's salary/wages			
Less: Withholding taxes			
FICA taxes			
Retirement programs			
Subtotal of deductions			
NET INCOME			
Other income			
TOTAL NET INCOME			

EXPENSES	PROJECTED	ACTUAL	DIFFERENCE
Fixed Expenses			
Rent/mortgage			
Retirement savings			
Scheduled fixed amortization			
Savings			
Debt repayment ____			
Debt repayment ____			
Debt repayment ____			
Debt repayment ____			
Debt repayment ____			
Other_____			
TOTAL FIXED EXPENSES			

	PROJECTED	ACTUAL	DIFFERENCE
Variable Expenses			
Food			
Utilities			
Phone			
Household operations			
Furnishings/equipment			
* Transportation/ vehicle maintenance			
Apparel			
Personal care			
Child care			
Recreation/ entertainment			
Special occasions			
Personal allowances			
Scheduled variable amortization			
Unscheduled variable amortization			
Savings			
Other _____			
TOTAL VARIABLE EXPENSES			
TOTAL EXPENSES			

PART 3

Yours, Mine, Ours

During the twentieth century, the main purpose for the family changed. Back in the days when most families lived on farms, the primary function of the family was survival through *production,* so the needs of the whole family took precedence over the needs of individuals. In contrast, in today's industrial society, families are *consumption* oriented, and the needs of individuals often take precedence over the preservation of the family. More and more family members tend to think of resources and belongings as "yours," "mine," or "ours."

Some of the factors that contribute to this perspective

were explored in Part 1 and Part 2 of this book. Part 1 examines how our personalities and families of origin affect our relationships and the way we manage our finances.

Part 2 discusses financial principles that can lead us into and out of financial problems, and emphasizes principles of avoiding, managing, and reducing debt.

Part 3 combines this information and applies it in ways designed to enhance your financial and personal relationships, and to address real-life situations typically faced by today's families.

CHAPTER **9**

LIFE BY DESIGN

If you were to think back on all the unexpected challenges that have already occurred in your life, the very thought of "designing" your life may appear to be an effort in futility. Life may often seem to be an endless series of challenges, interrupted by an occasional crisis. This pattern seems to be especially true with regard to finances and relationships; as soon as you have successfully coped with one crisis, a new challenge comes crashing down.

After successfully coping with these challenges, you may justifiably experience a feeling of inner pride—of self-confidence and independence that comes from being self-reliant. You may also experience a feeling of relief, a reevaluation of your limitations and capabilities, and in many cases a redirecting of your resources toward growing rather than merely maintaining. This redirected energy often allows you to become more creative, more courageous—life indeed becomes worth living.

Life by Design versus Life by Default

Some of this redirected energy can be aimed at attaining greater harmony among establishing your values, setting your goals, and controlling your behavior—essential elements to being able to live your life by design rather than by default. You can now come closer to being, as William Henley suggested in his 1875 poem "Invictus," the master of your fate.

In the fell clutch of circumstance
I have not winced or cried aloud.
Under the bludgeonings of chance
My head is bloody, but unbowed. . . .
It matters not how strait the gate,
How charged with punishments the scroll,
I am the master of my fate:
I am the captain of my soul.[1]

Living your life by design means careful planning and preparation to take advantage of opportunity rather than merely relying on luck or chance. In fact, one definition of good luck is "when preparation meets opportunity." For example, an office worker might comment, "Boy, was Carol lucky to get transferred to the Paris office." But if he were to look behind the scenes, he would find that Carol had studied French for five years. When the opportunity came to work in the Paris office, she was prepared. Carol was living a life by design. She knew where she wanted to go and what she needed to do to get there.

When you live your life by default, you allow your destiny to be determined by the fickleness of fate. Think how vague and unfocused such a life would be. Imagine asking someone you had just met, "How did you end up living here?" and hearing the reply, "About 12 years ago, I was traveling through this part of the country in my old station wagon. This is where the transmission went out—and I've been here ever since." Life by default often means standing still, waiting for the next roll of the dice.

Knowing where you are, however, is not as important as knowing where you are headed. In 1858, Oliver Wendell Holmes, the distinguished Supreme Court justice, said, "I find the great thing in this world is not so much where we stand, as in what direction we are moving; to reach the port of heaven, we must sail sometimes with the wind and sometimes against it—but we must sail, and not drift, nor lie at anchor."[2]

As you may have discovered, facing heavy debt can often seem like being stranded on a sandbar—it leaves you unable to respond to the winds of change, to take advantage of opportunities that come your way. Being free of debt, on the other hand, leaves you free to choose, to save or spend, to buy or sell, to stay or move, to change jobs or keep the one you have. Financial freedom enhances a very important part of your personal life—freedom of choice.

Financial Freedom

Chapter 1's financial principles are fundamental to basic thinking about financial management decisions. Principles 7 through 10, in particular, contain advice that underlies financial freedom. Much of this advice concerns reframing—changing your attitudes and outlook so that, by taking charge of your circumstances, you can become the master of your financial fate, the captain of your spending soul.

Spend Less, Need Less

Principle 7 states, *Financial freedom is more often the result of decreased spending than of increased income.* As chapter 6 explains, it is very difficult to *earn* your way out of debt. You would have to increase your income by as much as $1,000 before deducting taxes to achieve the same result as reducing your debt load by only $600.

For example, remember Alberto and Mendy from chapter 1? They were reasonably frugal, but their money seemed to "just disappear" with not a lot to show for it. They were getting by, but they weren't getting ahead. One month, after paying the bills and again having almost nothing left to live on, the two decided to take drastic measures. Should Alberto get a second job, or should they decrease their spending? They decided to cut back on just about everything in an attempt to increase their available finances.

They rode the bus to work and school instead of driving ($100 spent on gas – $40 bus fare = $60 savings per month). They went to $1.50 movies instead of $7 movies ($14 per movie twice a month would come to $28 – $6 for discount movies = $22 savings). They bought inexpensive steaks and had a candlelight dinner at home instead of going to a restaurant ($25 savings). They wore sweaters at home instead of turning up the thermostat ($15 savings). Alberto brown-bagged lunch instead of eating out ($50 savings). Mendy wrote letters instead of making long-distance calls ($20 savings). Alberto bought a secondhand tool instead of a new one ($15 savings).

Their efforts resulted in a $207 reduction in expenditures—money they could use to save for a new home, go on a vacation, or do whatever else they desired. If Alberto had taken a second job, he would have had to make around $325 per month in new earnings to clear that $205—an additional $4,000 in earnings to obtain an additional $2,460 per year to spend. For many of us, as for Alberto and Mendy, it may be easier to save $2,460 by using good home economics than to earn an extra $4,000.

Spending Inflation

Unfortunately, many families practice the opposite of Principle 7: They try to achieve financial freedom by increasing their income. In 1970 the nation's total consumer debt was $131.6 billion; by 1980, it had grown to $350 billion. By 1988 it was $730 billion, and by 1996 it was a whopping $1.2 *trillion.* Credit card debt alone increased from $55 billion in 1980 to a projected $783 billion in 2000. Family income increased during the past few decades, but the amount families spent increased even faster.[3]

Many families decided that the ever-increasing debt load meant only one thing: "We just can't make it on one income any more." Perhaps it would have been more accurate to say, "We just can't continue to sustain our higher level of spending on one income."

In 1955, the median family income was $17,693 (in 1986 dollars) with only the husband working. By 1986, the median family income (with only the husband working) had grown to $24,390—more than a 40 percent increase after adjusting for inflation.[4] For a variety of reasons, an ever-increasing number of wives and mothers entered the labor force, thereby creating the "dual-income family." In 1995, the dual-income family's median income (with husband and wife working full time) was $53,309.[5] This combined income was over *three times* the income their parents needed to raise their families in 1955, and almost twice the 1995 median income for families in which only the husband worked.[6]

Yet the belief persists that families can't make ends meet on just one income. That's because increasing debt load isn't the only financial challenge families have faced. The public's demand for ever-increasing government services has also taken its toll on the family pocketbook. Today, the average American family pays more in federal, state, and local taxes than for food, clothing, transportation, and housing combined. Breadwinners must work three hours of every eight-hour workday just to pay their tax bills.

We have lost sight of what previous generations spent to raise a family and replaced those standards with unrealistic expectations regarding higher living standards and increased government services. Do we really need extra income and government, or do we just need to take a better look at *wanting less?*

Gratitude Brings Perspective

We cannot judge how financially satisfied people are simply by looking at how much money they make. The degree of satisfaction we feel can often depend as much on what we *have* as on how much we *earn*. Similarly, what we *want* may be more important to financial satisfaction than what *needs have already been met.* If our family wants exceed our family income, the income will be inadequate—regardless of its level or how much it increases. Therefore, decreasing wants and expectations can be as important as increasing income.

Perhaps, however, you have already come to the conclusion that enough is enough and you no longer wish to participate in the "rat race." You have determined what is sufficient for your needs (see chapter 6) and want to devote your energy to something besides earning the almighty dollar or obtaining an unending array of worldly goods. If you do decide to pull out of the "never-ending quest," you might find that your lot in life is not all that bad.

Be grateful for what you have, advises Principle 8. One instructor in a sociology course asked a class three questions:

1. Do you own more than one pair of shoes?
2. Do you expect to eat more than just one kind of food each day?
3. Do you have access to your own personal form of transportation?

The instructor then pointed out that if you could answer yes to these three questions, you would be—financially—among *the top 10 percent of all the people who have ever lived on earth!* Comparing yourself to others on the planet and throughout history instead of with the people across the street can place you in a pretty good light. After all, don't we all start off and end the same? "Naked came I out of my mother's womb, and naked shall I return thither" (Job 1:21).

Freebie Exercise

Remember Principle 9? *The best things in life are free.* Fortunately, life offers a great number of pleasurable things. The enjoyment you find depends a lot more on your attitude than on your wealth. The following exercise is designed to help you, and those you love, rediscover some inexpensive yet fun activities.

List 20 activities that you consider fun or that have made you happy. You may enjoy snowball fights, for example, or diving into piles of autumn leaves, walking by a stream, going to foreign films, talking to a friend, reading a good book, going to a sports event, attending a concert, traveling, gardening, fishing, taking guitar lessons, and so on. Complete your list before reading any further.

Now place a heart next to those activities you prefer to do with others. Complete this part of the exercise before going on. Next, place a $ next to those activities that cost more than $10 per person to do. Complete this part of the exercise before proceeding.

Now review your list. If you are like most people, you will find you prefer to do about one-third to one-half of your favorite activities with another person. Even more important, you may discover that most of the things you associate with being truly happy cost less than $10 or are absolutely free. These you can call your *freebies.*

This exercise illustrates that you don't need a lot of money to be happy. You need enough money to take care of your basic needs, a little more to take care of some of your wants and to add a certain degree of quality to your life, and a bit more to give you a sense of security. Money beyond these requirements will not necessarily bring you more happiness.

Great differences exist between living by design and living by default. Financial freedom, as opposed to financial independence, is possible if we make proper choices. One of those choices is to reduce spending, which is often easier than increasing income. An examination of our earning and spending habits will help us to know whether our need for a second income is real or merely perceived. We can also choose to be grateful for what we have, stop perpetually wanting more, and remember that "the best things in life are free."

NOTES

1. Henley, 1978, 206.
2. Holmes, 1858, 228.
3. U.S. Department of Commerce, 1990a.
4. U.S. Department of Commerce, 1990b.
5. U.S. Department of Commerce, 1996a.
6. U.S. Department of Commerce, 1996b.

CHAPTER 10

FINANCIAL ISSUES AND FAMILY TYPES

Today's world includes several types of families: those considered "intact," those headed by single parents, and those that are "blended" (with children from previous marriages). To understand the diverse needs of each group, we must examine them from a modern, as well as traditional, perspective. Each type of family presents unique financial and interpersonal challenges that affect each family member's well-being and that call for specific coping skills.

Today's families need help balancing their financial ledgers as well as their "emotional" ledgers. Emotional ledgers reflect the personal losses and gains associated with marriage, divorce, widowhood, single parenting, and remarriage. Many who wish to be self-reliant find themselves dependent on the supplemental income of a former spouse, court-ordered child support, or welfare.

Measuring a Family's Economic Well-Being

It is important to keep in mind that a family's economic well-being alone does not provide a complete picture of overall well-being. A more complete perspective of how well a family is doing includes a view of their emotional well-being and of the quality of their interpersonal relationships. The degree of cordiality present among family members, however, can be strongly influenced by family economics—not necessarily by the size of the family income but by the family's *attitude* toward this income.

In many cases, the size of the family income does not even become an issue unless the emotional needs of the children are not being met. For those who have been reared in a loving family, it is not uncommon for them to exclaim as adults, "I never knew we were as poor as we were until I grew up and left home." Or "We had to scrimp a little now and then, but I thought we were just a middle-class family until we went over the particulars of Mom and Dad's will." They may even comment, "I'd see kids at school that I considered rich; they wore more expensive clothes than I did, for example. But I didn't feel *poor*—just not as well off as they were."

But for children whose needs for love and attention are not being met—whether at home or in outside relationships—being able to *buy* things can become extremely important. Remember Principle 6: *You can never get enough of what you don't need because what you don't need can never satisfy you.* A supporting maxim might be, "Most children can survive poverty, but only a few can survive wealth."

Nevertheless, a family's economic well-being is important, and it is influenced by both the amount of income available and the size of the family. Financial counselors commonly use two methods to determine a family's economic well-being: total family income and income-to-need ratios.

Total Family Income

Total family income compares a family's income to a national norm. In 1994, the median income for *all* families (including single-wage-earner, dual-wage-earner, and single-parent families) was $38,782. For white families, the median income was $40,884; for African-American families, $24,698; and for Hispanic families, $24,318. For all *married* families, the median income in 1994 was $44,959; for dual-income families it was almost $8,500 greater.

The median income for single-parent families (female head of household with no husband present) was only $18,236. Incomes for black and Hispanic families were even lower (see Table 10.1, page 175). In 1995, the average poverty threshold for a family of four was $15,569.[1] Family income is considered to be adequate when it is twice the poverty level for a family of a given size.

Income-to-Need Ratio

The income-to-need ratio for a family is determined by dividing a family's income by the poverty threshold for a family of a given size (see Table 10.2). For example, the income-to-need ratio for a family of four with an income of $19,500 can be figured by dividing $19,500 by $15,569: 19,500/15,569 = 1.25. The higher the ratio, the better the family is doing financially.

TABLE 10.1—1994 MEDIAN FAMILY INCOME

	ALL FAMILIES	WHITE	HISPANIC	AFRICAN AMERICAN
All configurations	$38,782	$40,884	$24,318	$24,698
Married	$44,959	$45,474	$29,621	$40,432
Dual-income	$53,309	$53,977	$38,559	$47,235
Single-parent (female)	$18,236	$20,795	$12,117	$13,943

Adapted from *Money Income of Families—Median Family Income in Constant (1994) Dollars* (p. 471), by U.S. Department of Commerce, Bureau of the Census, 1996, Washington, D.C.: U.S. Government Printing Office.

Single-Wage-Earner Families

A single-wage-earner family is a *two-parent* family in which only one parent earns income. Interestingly, and perhaps as a sign of the times, only about 10 percent of families in the United States currently fit the definition of the "traditional family," with the husband the sole breadwinner and the wife at home with two or more children.[2]

Some of the questions confronting single-wage-earner families are: Who will control the finances and decide how money will be spent? How will the needs and wants of individual family members be met? How will value conflicts be handled?

TABLE 10.2—1995 POVERTY THRESHOLDS

NUMBER OF PERSONS IN FAMILY	THRESHOLD IN DOLLARS
1	$ 7,763
2	9,933
3	12,158
4	15,569

5	18,408
6	20,804
7	23,552
8	26,237
9	31,280

Adapted from *Poverty in the United States*, 1995, p. 476, by U.S. Department of Commerce, Bureau of the Census, 1996, Washington, D.C.: U.S. Government Printing Office.

Income-Management Systems Used by Single-Wage-Earner Families

Single-wage-earner families usually use either the *managing-spouse system* or the *allowance system* to manage their income.[3]

With the managing-spouse system, (1) the wage earner turns all earnings over to the spouse, (2) the spouse is responsible for managing the finances and paying all the bills, and (3) the manager spouse returns some personal spending money to the wage earner. The managing-spouse system is frequently used among lower-income families, with the husband as wage earner and the wife as managing spouse. In a slight variation on this income-management system, the wage earner withholds personal spending money before turning the earnings over to the managing spouse. (However, in some instances, the wage earner has been known to deceive the managing spouse by working overtime without turning over the extra money.)

With the allowance system, the wage earner (1) deposits earnings in the checking account, (2) pays the larger bills, and (3) gives the non-wage earner an allowance to meet regular housekeeping obligations. The allowance system seems to be more common among middle- and high-income families. Under this system, the wage earner pays the mortgage and major loans and makes investments. After meeting these obligations, the wage earner usually determines the size of the household allowance, which the non-wage earner frequently considers to be insufficient. Additional frustration occurs when income increases without a corresponding increase in the household allowance.

Family-of-Origin Rules

As chapter 2 points out, because each spouse is reared in a different family of origin, each brings to the marriage a different set of rules about how finances should be handled. Such differences, if not resolved, can become a constant source of contention.

To effectively cope with differences, both partners should share how finances were handled in their family. Using Worksheet 2.1, chapter 2, decide which rules are most important, which ones you want to include in your current family, and what compromises and accommodations you need to make.

Martin and Marina's situation can be used as an illustration of the problems that can result from different rules of family finances. Martin, filled with frustration, tries again to point out what he thought was obvious to every rational human being but his wife: "Marina, we cannot spend money we don't have. That credit card is to be used only in an emergency, not to buy things just because they happen to be on sale."

Marina, also upset, responds defensively, "Well, I can't run the house on what little you give me each month. Isaac made the basketball team and needed a pair of shoes."

Martin pounds his fist on his knee and mutters loudly enough to be heard, "My dad warned me that if I didn't hold a firm grip on the finances, you'd put us in the poorhouse. Well, I'm not going to let that happen. Mom never used a credit card in her life. She managed on what Dad gave her and did a darned good job of it. If she did it, you can do it."

Marina stands for a moment in an absolute state of shock. When she recovers, she speaks slowly and deliberately. "I have no intention of being treated the way your father treated your mother. My mom and dad shared everything on an equal basis, including money. They had a joint checking account, and each one carried a checkbook. My mother *never* had to beg for money, and I'm not about to start either."

Martin, somewhat unnerved by Marina's counterattack, says in a much calmer voice, "Well, then, what *are* we going to do?"

Grasping the opportunity, Marina presents her recommendation. "For one thing, if I had my own checkbook I wouldn't even consider using a credit card. My parents didn't like credit cards any more than yours did."

Martin protests, "If we both had checkbooks, we'd end up bouncing checks all over the place."

Marina shakes her head and replies, "Not if we communicate with each other."

Martin is still a little reluctant—after all, his father was always the one who wrote the checks. But what Marina has said makes sense, and it could resolve the credit card issue. "I'm not sure how both of us having checkbooks is going to work out, but I guess it's worth a try. My mom did tell me I was marrying a gal with a head on her shoulders, and if I didn't listen to you, she'd come over and talk some sense into me."

Anger never justifies demeaning a loved one. Appropriately expressing your concerns and trying to understand your partner's perspective and problems can be a far more effective means of bringing about change.

Preferential Treatment

If some members of the family believe that others receive preferential treatment when it comes to finances, they can become jealous and argumentative. To reduce these feelings, analyze your distribution of financial-managerial tasks—shopping for groceries, buying clothes, purchasing new or used cars, preparing the monthly budget, paying the bills, cashing checks, making deposits, earning income, and so on (see Worksheet 2.6, chapter 2). Determine who is responsible for which tasks and whether each person is satisfied with the current arrangement. Be sure to discuss how each family member perceives the fairness of the task distribution.

In addition, find out if family members feel that different standards or rules apply to members according to age or ability to earn money. Do the older children get a larger allowance than the younger ones? Do the younger children get more help because they aren't old enough to work? Similarly, conflicts often appear when parents pay for dance lessons but not for karate lessons, or when they support those who want to go to college but not those who want to learn a trade.

Favoritism is more perceived rather than real; therefore, you have to determine what you can do not only to ensure fair treatment but also to help family members perceive that they are being treated equally (see *Reframing*, chapter 4). You may also need to negotiate a settlement (see *Negotiations*, chapter 4).

Dual-Income Families

In a dual-income family, both spouses are present, and both work either part time or full time. The decision to have both husband and wife work outside the home can be a sensitive one for many households. However, the number of dual-income families has grown for some time as ever-increasing economic pressures have forced both the husband and the wife into the workforce.

In 1890, women made up only 17 percent of the workforce. By 1980, that figure had jumped to 51.5 percent. By 1996, 61 percent of the U.S. labor force was female. During the same period, the percentage of wage-producing women rose from 4.5 percent in 1890 to 28 percent in 1960 to 67 percent in 1996.[4]

Marital Stress in Dual-Income Families

As you might have guessed, the income-management system to be used in the dual-income family is an important decision. Issues of allocation and control often loom large: Who has claim on which income? How will the incomes be allocated to meet expenditures? How will the personal needs of both partners be satisfied? How might differences in earnings between partners affect self-esteem, personal interaction, and sharing of household responsibilities?

Marital stress is often a result of both partners working outside the home. As a result, the advantages of a second income may not be as great as they seem at first glance. Having a second income does not necessarily mean a great increase in funds. As a rule-of-thumb, because of the additional deductions and costs associated with earning a second income, *only about one-third* of the gross amount of this income actually comes home with you. If your family's second income were $15,000, for example, you could expect only about a $5,000 increase in the amount of money available for family use. The amount actually realized will vary in accordance with family income levels, but it is almost always less than you expected.

Use Worksheet 10.1 (page 192) to calculate the *net income effects* of a second income on your family. Realize, however, that this worksheet will *not* measure the time you could have spent with your spouse or children instead of working, nor will it measure the toll taken in fatigue, health, and emotional well-being. It may be worthwhile to evaluate exactly what you gain from the extra income when compared to what you lose.

Allocation and Control

Allocation and control conflicts—common in dual-income families—usually center more on the way resources are allocated than on how much there is to allocate. For example, one spouse might exclaim, "I ought to be able to afford an exercise bike with the kind of money I make, let alone what the two of us make. The bike only costs $184. I want someone to tell me where all my money's going. I'm tired of working and having nothing to show for it." Though items and amounts differ, this scenario is a fairly typical financial argument in a dual-income family (see *Love versus Power*, chapter 3).

This tendency to argue over things is futile. Imagine watching two children through the porthole of a ship. They are fighting over what one has and the other wants. You want them to stop, so you open the door to their stateroom and try to convince them that the things they are arguing over don't really matter because they won't be able to take anything off the ship. They remain unconvinced. What they don't realize is that their ship, the *Titanic*, has just struck an iceberg.

Like most other families, dual-income families are affected by the principle of *scarcity:* any allocation of resources to one end implies that fewer resources will be available for other ends. Family members need to work together so that resource allocation generates (1) the greatest benefits (2) for the most people (3) at the least cost. In order to achieve this, you should observe the fundamental principles of negotiating: First, remember that negotiations are designed to produce a mutually beneficial outcome, not a one-sided victory. Second, cooperate rather than compete. Third, communicate with each other in a way that safeguards one another's self-esteem.

Arguments often occur when couples have inaccurate or incomplete information. They may not know what their actual income is, what their actual costs are, how much credit they have used, or how much credit they can handle. Their arguments are based on what each *perceives* is happening with their finances (see *Your Perceived Budget*, chapter 8). They may criticize, blame, and find fault with each other until each decides to take care of his or her own money and his or her own expenses. They develop a "yours, mine, and ours" attitude toward income distribution, which can create feelings of emotional distance between partners.

Negative feelings toward income distribution is not the only cause of emotional distancing. Distribution of the responsibilities of earning an income and of running a household can also affect the quality of the marriage and the happiness of the individual partners. In most cases, wives who work outside the home contribute more to household chores than do their husbands, and the more a husband earns in comparison to what his wife makes, the less his contribution to household chores. Equitable distribution of financial and household responsibilities in marriage depends on effective communication and the ability to understand the difference between consenting to be useful or charitable, and being exploited (see *Relationships and Financial Priorities,* chapter 3). To exploit others is to use them without their complete emotional and intellectual consent or to use them without sufficient consideration for their welfare. It seems that couples enjoy a greater degree of marital satisfaction when both spouses are involved in making financial decisions.[5]

Divorce in Dual-Income Families

One of the more measurable consequences of the increase in the number of dual-income families and the resulting increase in family stress is divorce. A survey of census reports showed that in states where more married women work full time, the divorce rate is higher. In states where more married women work part time, the divorce rate is lower.[6]

The correlation between divorce rates and the number of hours married women work seems to be supported by other research findings as well.[7] The number of hours away from home has a greater impact on the probability of divorce than the size of the woman's earnings. This relationship is strongest among middle-income families and those in which the husband disapproves of the wife's employment. (However, these researchers did not consider the question of how a reduction in hours worked *by husbands* in dual-income families might reduce marital stress.)

It is interesting to note that divorce is no more likely in a dual-income couple than in a single-income couple (in which the husband works) if the wife earns an above-average income and the husband approves highly of her career. But in cases where the wife earns more than her husband, or the husband is periodically unemployed, the probability of divorce is higher.[8]

Marital success, like individual happiness, depends more on the degree of satisfaction derived from the money earned than on the actual amount. Also, it seems that marital stability increases with the number of assets accumulated rather than with increases in income.[9] It can be quite frustrating for both spouses to work hard over a period of years and then have nothing to show for their labor.

Dual-Career Families

A special category of the dual-income family is the dual-career family. One of the distinctions between the two is that in the dual-income family, the wife usually views work merely as a source of economic security without a long-term career goal in mind. The woman who is career oriented, however, views work as a sequence of promotions with clearly organized goals and time frames for reaching certain milestones.[10]

Dual-career families tend to experience greater financial stress than either single-wage-earner or dual-income families—often because of gender differences in pay, job opportunities, and career advancement. Additional stress can occur as a result of jealousy or required relocation. Dual-career families also experience a great deal of emotional stress as the breadwinners find themselves torn between the desire to fulfill personal ambitions and the expectations of spouses and children. Inequality between husband and wife with regard to sharing household responsibilities can be especially sensitive. In addition, concerns arise over personal identity, self-esteem, and society's role expectations.[11] Primary problems facing dual-career families include:

1. Gender-based discrimination that results in differences in pay, job opportunities, and career advancement.

2. Persistent inequality between husband and wife with regard to sharing household responsibilities.

3. Additional expenses for full- or part-time housekeeping, gardening, and child care.

4. Relocation that is not compatible with the other spouse's career.

5. Potential for professional competition and jealousy.

Income-Management Systems Used by Dual-Income and Dual-Career Families

The two income management systems most commonly used by dual-income/dual-career families are the *shared-management system* and the *independent-management system.*[12]

In the shared-management system, (1) both incomes are deposited in a joint account, (2) both partners have equal access to this account, (3) both assume responsibility for managing this account, and (4) household expenditures are randomly assumed by either spouse. Under this system, *both* partners share in managerial tasks. Both discuss allocation issues and try to arrive at a consensus for distribution of funds.

Studies show that marriages with this kind of equal control over financial decisions (either making joint decisions or agreeing that each partner assumes responsibility for specific financial tasks) have the least amount of conflict.[13] (These findings support the recommendation in chapter 3 that dominance/submission issues be viewed from the perspective of reciprocal roles of responsibility between equals rather than from a position of superiority/inferiority.)

One of the benefits of the shared-management system is that it confronts problems of trust. Trust issues arise when one spouse tries to hide earnings from the other spouse, or when one spouse suspects the other of juggling the books or keeping income for personal use. The shared-management system is, in fact, based on trust. Since either spouse can write checks on the single account—and wipe it out if he or she wants to—this system requires mutual trust and mature, responsible behavior.

Here is a common modification of this system: (1) one spouse assumes responsibility for managing the joint account and family expenditures, and (2) this spouse assigns specific incomes to specific expenditures. The manager can be either husband or wife, and incomes are usually assigned to expenses on the basis of convenience. For instance, if one spouse is paid weekly, those checks might be assigned to buying food, gasoline for the cars, entertainment, and other cash expenses. If the other spouse is paid on a monthly basis, that income could be assigned to mortgage, loan, and utility payments.

In the *independent-management system,* (1) the income of each spouse is deposited in a separate account, (2) neither spouse has access to all of the income, (3) specific financial obligations are assigned to each spouse, and (4) each spouse's income is treated as personal money. One spouse might be responsible for paying the mortgage, while the other might be responsible for the utilities. Each might be responsible for his or her own car payments, insurance payments, and car repairs. However, should one spouse be unable to meet obligations, the couple transfers funds on a temporary or permanent basis from one account to the other.

One of the advantages of this system is that it provides clear, uncluttered records for income tax purposes. It is also a convenient way of providing income/expenditure stability when one of the incomes is variable due to commissions, seasonal work, and so forth.

Single-Parent Families

In a single-parent family, one parent is absent because of divorce, separation, or death—or there was no marriage in the first place. For the single parent, poverty is often unavoidable, with the vast majority of the financial and emotional responsibility for rearing children falling on the mother. Unfortunately, many fathers, once they are *legally* divorced, seem to think that they no longer have a financial obligation for the children they helped to produce. Only about 50 percent of ex-husbands actually make full child-support payments as ordered by the courts, while 25 percent make only partial payments.[14] As a result, most women entitled to child support receive little or no payments. Adding injury to insult are a great many extra costs associated with being a single parent, such as child care, loss of wages due to time off to care for children, and so forth. Being a single parent usually means dealing with feelings of anger, frustration, and resentment about your situation. On the positive side, being a single parent can also provide opportunities for the development of a greater sense of self-reliance and independence.

Enmeshment

One of the most common problems associated with being a single parent is a reduction in the emotional separateness between parent and child. After a divorce or death, the parent and child often look to each other to satisfy their emotional needs. As a result, they can become *enmeshed*.

People are enmeshed when they become so dependent on each other that it is unclear where one person's identity ends and the other person's begins. It is no longer clear whether a need or emotion belongs to one person or the other. For example, a single parent may believe that a child wants a new toy, when actually it is the *parent* who wants to buy the child a new toy. Similarly, single parents may suffer for what they perceive to be the child's loneliness and deprivation, when in fact these are their own feelings. This lack of emotional separateness can have a great effect on how finances are managed.

When a child in an economically solvent family says, "I don't want hamburger for dinner," the parents will probably think that the child simply does not feel like eating hamburger and would rather eat hot dogs or spaghetti. But to a single parent who is under emotional and financial stress and who is still trying to adjust to a lower standard of living, the child's statement might imply, "I don't like the way we eat any more. I want to eat stuff like we used to eat." The parent may then reply to the hamburger rejection with, "I know it's been hard on you kids since the divorce, but I'm doing the best I can."

To stop being enmeshed, family members need to assume personal responsibility for their own feelings, appropriately expressing them and trusting that other family members will cope with them. They need to accept the fact that their family is not perfect, and they must recognize that mistakes will be made and feelings will be hurt even if family members do their best to be responsible and considerate. They need to acknowledge that each person can belong to the family and still develop some degree of independence.

Doing Without for the Children's Sake

The financial strain that often accompanies single parenthood can worsen problems of enmeshment and make parents feel that they need to deprive themselves for their children's sake. Continually setting aside your own needs in favor of your children's needs may eventually create feelings of resentment and jealousy. In order to avoid this, set aside for yourself some percentage of the money you intend to spend on the children. For example, if you plan to spend $100 for children's clothing, you should either spend $10, $25, or $50 of that money on your own clothing or, if you can afford it, spend $100 on the children and an additional $10, $25, or $50 on yourself.

Most parents are often willing to sacrifice for the sake of their children, but this seems to be especially true for single parents. Because they have less money to go around, they often put their own needs last. Typical single mothers, for example, buy their children new school clothes each year but wear the same things themselves year after year. These single parents may be sending a different message to their children than they think they are sending. Perhaps their children will think, "Golly, Mom, we can hardly wait to grow up. Then we can wear rags like you, and eat the scraps off other people's plates."

This exaggerated example may seem strong, but the point is that parents have needs too. Children need to understand that. If parents show respect for themselves, their children will more likely show them respect. Giving children everything they want while you do without is not love; it is martyrdom. In *The Road Less Traveled*, M. Scott Peck reminds us that "Love is not simply giving; it is *judiciously* giving and judiciously withholding as well."[15]

Things and Relationships

As noted in chapter 5, feelings often influence purchases. For example, single parents might buy things for their children in an attempt to compensate for the loss of the other parent, the amount of time the single parent is at work, or the family's lower economic status. But in most cases, the family can substantially reduce the "need" to acquire material things by developing warm, loving relationships among themselves. If you are buying things for the children to let them know that you care about them, just try telling them directly.

Perhaps a child asks for a new bicycle. Her harried mother responds, "Do you think I'm made of money? I've barely got enough to pay for the rent, let alone pay for a bicycle!" The child will most likely go away feeling resentful, guilty for having upset her mother, who is obviously overburdened already and convinced that nobody cares about her feelings.

Now picture the same scenario with a different parental response. This time the mother focuses on her daughter's feelings rather than on the cost of the bicycle and responds, "I've had a feeling that you might be wanting a new bicycle, and I've been trying to juggle our budget to see if there is any way we might be able to buy one. I've got a pretty good idea how much having a bicycle would mean to you, but it just doesn't look like we can afford one right now. However, *I want* you to have a new bicycle, and I will do everything I can to make it happen."

The parent still cannot afford to buy a new bicycle, but now the daughter does not question her importance or whether someone cares about her feelings. This approach affords some excellent opportunities to teach family goal-setting policies and effective problem-solving techniques. This approach also gives the parent an opportunity to teach the child how to cope with feelings associated with delayed gratification. In other words, instead of selfishly focusing on stress and problems, the parent has created a teaching moment.

Blended Families

A blended family, or stepfamily, results from a remarriage in which one or both partners bring children from a previous relationship. As in other two-spouse families, the income-management system is an important consideration. Since the financial demands of a blended family are typically more complex than those of an original marriage, problems related to allocation of resources are correspondingly more stressful. Questions quickly arise with regard to allocation and control. For example, how can the divorced husband remarry and meet the needs of two families unless he asks his new wife to also work? How will the husband meet the health care and educational needs of the children? How will the new couple spend child support? How will the spouses handle adoption and the subsequent loss of child support? How will they deal with perceptions of favoritism and neglect? How will they pay for debts acquired during the previous marriage? How will they redistribute, dispose of, or supervise assets acquired before the current marriage? What steps should they take regarding estate planning to protect the interests of all family members?

Family Boundaries

In a blended family, members from one side almost always think that members from the other side play favorites or neglect them in relationships and with resources. One reason for this is that blended families find it difficult to define family boundaries.[16] Family boundaries distinguish between who is "family" and who is not. Those who are considered family have certain privileges and rights that others do not have. Determining family boundaries in a blended family can become a very complex task. Do the family boundaries include:

Children from the previous marriages living *within* the current household?

Children from the previous marriages living *outside* the current household?

Children from the current marriage?

Only blood-related members (even if none of them are living with the current family)?

Only those with the same last name (natural or adopted)?

Everyone currently living in the same house?

It is important to resolve these issues, because family boundaries can have as significant an impact on allocation of financial support as can the courts. The complexity of allocation problems often centers on the issue of fairness. Can favoritism be avoided as parents decide whose money goes to which child for what purpose.

For example, John and Sally have divorced. Sally takes custody of the children and marries Raymond, who is also divorced and has custody of his children. Sally and Raymond thus create a blended family. John also remarries. His new wife, Michelle, also has children over whom she has custody.

If John were to buy his children new winter coats (even though he doesn't have custody), while the children from Michelle's previous marriage had to wear hand-me-downs, Michelle's children would naturally ask, "How come they get new coats and we don't?" Raymond's children could ask the same question. In either situation, the answer to their question would undoubtedly draw cries of "That's not fair!"

Old Debts and Liabilities

Unless debts that originated in a former marriage are paid off, they can be a source of perpetual marital discord. As constant reminders of unpleasant feelings associated with the previous marriage, old debts and liabilities can cause emotional turmoil and resentment in the new relationship. For example, a wife might be quite willing to help pay off her new husband's car (part of the assets he brings to the current marriage), yet be adamantly opposed to making payments on his ex-wife's car. "Every time I write out a check for her car, I get so upset. I have to ride the bus to work while she drives around in a fancy car. It's just not fair."

Couples could significantly reduce tension levels by determining which debts generate the most resentment and contention, and paying them off as soon as possible. It is helpful to arrange an electronic transfer of payments from one bank to another so that it's not necessary to write checks and be repeatedly reminded of a sore spot (see *Steps to Take to Resolve a Financial Crisis,* chapter 6).

Previously Acquired Assets

When people remarry, they bring not only debts and liabilities but assets as well. Differences in the perceived value of assets brought into a marriage can cause contention and mistrust in blended families.

Assets are often divided by legal judgments in divorce proceedings. Sometimes the property a partner brings to a new marriage may represent the only thing worth salvaging from the previous marriage. As a consequence, the partner who contributes the property may be possessive of it and worry about who can use it and how it can be used. If one spouse does not appreciate the intrinsic value of the other's possessions, he or she may appear insensitive. For example, a spouse might suggest, "Since we need a new car anyway, why don't we just sell your old pickup and get something decent?" The other, offended, might respond, "Don't even think such a thing! That 'old pickup' is the only thing that kept me sane in my first marriage—and the only thing she didn't get in the settlement. It's my reward for valor under combat conditions." Similar outcries can result from the husband using his wife's antique chairs for sawhorses.

If assets are relatively liquid, such as cash, stocks, or bonds, then problems can center on the proposed use of those assets: if and how they will be redistributed, whether they will be consumed, and, if so, at what rate and under whose supervision.

Financial Agreements

Most people develop attitudes toward assets and financial planning based not only on experience with their families of origin, but also on experience in their previous marriages. In order to avoid being exploited or making the same mistakes as in the past, each spouse may push for marital agreements that safeguard the way finances will be handled. If one spouse vigorously defends such agreements, the other may resent proposed restraints, conditions, or limits, and interpret them as a lack of love, trust, or commitment.

To encourage greater trust and commitment, each spouse in the new marriage should place at least *some* assets under joint supervision. This action should be taken in a gradual, progressive fashion. When a building's foundation is constructed out of concrete, the footings are poured first and then allowed to set for a while to gain strength before the floor is poured. In a similar fashion, each spouse might transfer a portion of assets from the "mine" account to the "ours" account. The couple might then let the situation rest for a period of time while building feelings of trust. Of course, some assets may remain forever separate, designated only for inheritance, emergency purposes, or as a source of security.

Income-Management Systems Used by Blended Families

Although there is no one right way to manage family finances, most blended-family couples seem to prefer the *shared-management system*. Dual-income blended families at high-income levels prefer the *independent-management system*.[17] Remarried couples may chose to use the *independent-management system* for a variety of reasons: each partner already has an established bank account; each is used to meeting certain financial obligations (most of which were assumed before the current marriage); and, unfortunately, each is likely to have been hurt financially in the previous marriage and may not be willing to be vulnerable again—at least for a while.

As with assets brought separately to the marriage, progressively blending incomes helps to overcome feelings of distance and lack of commitment. Pooling resources tends to encourage family unity, while keeping separate accounts may tend to promote personal autonomy and interfere with the integration of the blended family.

At first, you may wish to keep *all* of your income separate. But as time passes and you become more familiar as husband and wife, you may want to begin committing a portion of your income to a common account. Begin with about 10 percent of your earnings; then, as mutual feelings of trust increase, progressively devote a larger portion to the joint account. In this way, you can develop a sense of unity and commitment in your new family without the overwhelming fear of "losing everything" again.

NOTES

1. U.S. Department of Commerce, 1997a.
2. Smith, 1979.
3. McCrae, 1987; Paul, 1983.
4. U.S. Department of Commerce, 1997b.
5. Nye and Hoffman, 1974; Thomas, Albrecht, and White, 1984.
6. Yeh and Lester, 1987, 1988.
7. South and Spitze, 1985.
8. D'Amico, 1983; Moore and Hofferth, 1979.
9. Galligan and Bahr, 1978.
10. Rapoport and Rapoport, 1971.
11. Price-Bonham and Murphy, 1980.
12. Heath, 1986; McCrae, 1987; Pahl, 1983.
13. General Mills, 1975; Schaninger and Buss, 1986.
14. Taeber and Valdisera, 1986; U.S. Department of Commerece, 1990c.
15. Peck, 1978.
16. Ihinger-Tallman and Pasley, 1981; Pasley, 1987.
17. Heath, 1986.

WORKSHEET 10.1—NET INCOME EFFECTS OF A SECOND INCOME

EXPENSES ASSOCIATED WITH A SECOND INCOME

Federal income taxes (includes increases
from moving into higher tax bracket) _____

Social Security (if self-employed, this amount is
double what it would be if you were employed
by someone else) _____

State income taxes _____

Redundant insurance (many employers have a
mandatory participation group insurance plan that
may duplicate the coverage you already have
under the other wage earner's plan) _____

Additional transportation costs _____

Additional meal costs (meals at work, lunches out,
fast foods, frozen meals, and so on) _____

Child-care expenses _____

Household cleaning costs _____

Additional wardrobe and grooming costs _____

Total additional expenses _____

Gross monthly income _____

Minus additional expenses _____

NET BENEFITS _____

CHAPTER 11

FINANCIAL CHALLENGES AND THE LIFE CYCLE

Families are in a constant state of change; yet it is our inherent nature to resist change. Parents encourage their children to grow up while simultaneously discouraging them from growing up too fast. Families outgrow their homes and want to move to nicer places but are reluctant to leave familiar surroundings. Such dilemmas create internal conflict and strain as family members attempt to adjust to change. These dilemmas can be solved with knowledge, preparation, and skills adapted to each stage of our lives.

Family Life Cycle Stages

Many changes are predictable and identifiable, resulting from the transition from one stage in the life cycle to another. Psychologists and sociologists have proposed a number of theories concerning the stages we go through in life. Since our primary interest here is the dynamic between relationships and finances, we will divide the life cycle according to changes in age, marital status, and the presence of children in the home. (See Table 11.1, which also includes average income figures for each stage.)

Each stage in the life cycle has its own unique set of financial responsibilities or tasks. For example, during Stage 2, beginning families are primarily concerned with the costs of completing an education, creating a household, and establishing credit. A retired couple in Stage 6 is more likely concerned with adjusting to a lower income, obtaining adequate insurance protection, and transferring their estate.

TABLE 11.1—LIFE CYCLE STAGES

Stage	Age	Marital Status	Income
1	15–24	Single, with no children	$18,756
2	25–34	Married or single, with no children, or children ages 1–9	$36,020
3	35–44	Married or single, with children ages 10–19	$46,527
4	45–54	Married or single, launching children	$55,029
5	55–64	Married or single, with children launched	$45,264
6	65–over	Married or single, retired	$28,301

From *Statistical Abstract of the United States*, 1995 (p. 471), by U.S. Department of Commerce, Bureau of the Census, 1996, Washington, D.C.: U.S. Government Printing Office.

Fulfilling financial responsibilities can be difficult, and ample opportunities exist to make mistakes. Each stage in the life cycle offers its own financial obligations and common pitfalls.[1]

Stage 1: Single, with No Children

You are in Stage 1 of the life cycle if you are just out of school, not married, and have no children living with you. At this stage you are making some of your first major purchases (car, stereo, furniture, and so on). Many young people in this stage are prone to impulse buying; they see it, they want it, they buy it. Their income is still relatively low, and they begin establishing credit as soon as possible. Armed with an array of credit cards, many will soon find themselves overwhelmed with excessive debt and overextended credit. Caught up in the here-and-now life of the young, they give little thought to keeping financial records or making long-range goals. They make financial mistakes such as failing to file income taxes or spending money that was to go toward education. As a consequence, many young adults will remain financially dependent on their parents rather than becoming self-reliant; some will become so discouraged that they will turn to alcohol or drugs in a desperate attempt to escape the stresses of the financial mess they have created.

Living for Today, Preparing for Tomorrow

Remember that "free at last" feeling you had when you graduated from high school, and how impatient you were to get on with your life? Full-time employment, adult wages, and a big paycheck were your keys to freedom. You were finally going to buy the car of your dreams, rent your own apartment, and live a carefree life. All this seemed possible—unless, of course, you went to work for minimum wage in an unskilled, dead-end job. In that case, the only things you could afford were an old "junker" that didn't run half the time, a room with four weird roommates, and a box of saltine crackers to tide you over until payday.

Education is the answer to most problems of underemployment. In 1995, the average high school graduate earned $23,365 (male) or $12,046 (female) a year. The average college graduate earned $39,040 (male) or $24,065 (female), while someone with an advanced degree earned $66,257 (male) or $38,588 (female).[2]

If you keep school loans to a minimum, an education can really pay off. But if your educational loans become excessive, you can find yourself deeply in debt at the very time you're attempting to finance the needs of a new family and career. A $15,000 student loan with a 9 percent rate of interest over a ten-year payback period would cost you $7,800 in interest, and your monthly payments would be $190. You would have to earn around $325 each month (after deductions) just to clear enough to make those payments. This is equivalent to an almost $4,000 reduction in your yearly wages. To make up this difference you might be tempted to use your newly acquired credit cards.

The Credit Card Trap

Financial institutions often automatically mail credit cards to college graduates, hoping to cash in on their newly acquired higher incomes. Many graduates, having existed in a state of material deprivation for the past four or five years, experience a great deal of pent-up desire for consumption. To resolve this tension, they immediately use their newly acquired credit cards to acquire material goods.

Credit cards allow you to immediately enjoy things that may have taken your parents a lifetime to accumulate. And credit cards are more convenient than checks and safer than cash—what could be wrong with using them? When used wisely, credit cards can actually help you manage your finances efficiently—provided your monthly bills are paid on time and in full, and provided you use them only for emergencies or to purchase items that last longer than the payments.

However, young adults often lack the experience or discipline needed to properly manage an *open-ended line of credit.* Open-ended credit, or a revolving charge account, provides you with a pre-approved credit limit and flexible terms of repayment. The creditor allows you to pay off the loan with one payment, pay interest plus a larger-than-minimum portion of the principal, or pay interest plus a minimum portion of the principal. *Installment credit,* on the other hand, involves a prearranged schedule of repayment that is determined when the credit is approved.

Another difference between open-ended and installment credit is that many credit card applications do not undergo the same scrutiny that most loan applications do. As a result, young people often acquire numerous credit cards with a combined credit limit that far exceeds the amount they could qualify for through a bank installment loan (see *Stop Qualifying for Loans You Don't Really Qualify For,* chapter 6). You can accumulate a large amount of debt over a short period of time without fully realizing the magnitude of the financial problems you're generating.

As a young adult, you may tend to purchase assets that *consume income* or *depreciate* rapidly (cars, stereo equipment, boats, clothing, cheap furniture) instead of assets that *produce income* or have a chance to *appreciate* (stocks, real estate, IRAs, savings bonds). You may also be more inclined to spend a larger portion of your income on entertainment and recreation.

Looking Ahead

Many young adults are extremely responsible during this stage of their lives, planning and preparing well for their futures. But those who have been "living for the moment" will inevitably begin to feel frustrated when they fail to progress financially. Many reevaluate their spending habits, weighing how much they have earned over the past few years against how much they have to show for it.

Usually this reevaluation takes place when the single person starts thinking about getting married. Unfortunately, whether marrying for the first time or remarrying, many singles fail to prepare adequately for the financial challenges they will face. An ever-increasing percentage of singles approach marriage already deeply in debt.

Stage 2: Married or Single, with No Children or Children Ages 1–9

Stage 2 in the life cycle also includes singles with no children, because these singles are now older and in a higher income bracket. Nevertheless, this stage is commonly referred to as the beginning family stage, with the majority of people in this stage being married.

Most couples during this period adjust their relationships with their extended family to accommodate their new spouses. They focus time and energy on getting to know their partner's values and behaviors, and on adjusting to the arrival of children.

For some, the term *beginning family* carries an implied message that a beginning family is somehow "under construction" and therefore incomplete. But for many couples, being married with no children constitutes a finished product. And for a growing number of people, being "single with no children" constitutes a finished product.

For those who do have children, this stage has two distinct phases—before and after the arrival of children. Financial responsibilities and common financial mistakes are an integral part of both phases. One of the most common financial mistakes is the tendency to remain self-indulgent, using income to purchase expensive "toys" rather than accumulate assets needed for a growing family. Money spent on toys is not available to buy household goods, begin a savings program, or pay for education and career training. This failure to plan for the future can have long-term consequences, especially if the couple has not taken into consideration the possibility of having to live on just one income. In addition, such spending often leads to heavy indebtedness and conflicts over differences in values and goals.

Married or Single, with No Children

One of the most difficult transitions in life is from single life to marriage. The ritual and wording of the marriage ceremony may vary, but the intent is always the same: to set the couple apart from all others as an exclusive union entitled to special privileges and trusts not enjoyed by any other.

During this transition we realize that we must replace much of the autonomy we experienced as a single person with a sense of togetherness. Togetherness does not mean becoming inseparable, nor does it mean losing all personal identity. It does mean that both individuals must commit themselves to thoughtful consideration of the consequences of their actions on their partners. For example, as a single person, you are free to sell your house and move on impulse. But it is not advisable to greet an unsuspecting spouse with, "Hi, dear! Guess what? I sold the house today." Most spouses would consider such behavior an act of betrayal and insensitivity.

But many newly married couples may feel betrayed and deceived even without having the house sold out from under them. "Before we got married," they might say, "we used to go to nice restaurants, compliment each other on our appearance, and promise that things would only get better. But they haven't. Maybe being single was better!"

Much of the so-called "deception" regarding a partner's behavior before and after marriage can be explained by the mere fact that a new set of rules has come into play. As we progress through stages in our life cycle, we are governed by different rules—rules that we learned from our families of origin (see *Family Rules*, chapter 2). One set of rules governs how we should act while dating; a second set how we act after becoming engaged; a third set how to treat each other as husband and wife; a fourth set how to be a good father or a good mother; and a fifth set how we should rear our children.

If a husband no longer takes his wife to nice restaurants as often as he did when they were courting, he may simply be adhering to his family rules. He might explain to his wife that while he was engaged to her he followed the rules for being a fiancé, and after he married her he began following the rules for being a husband. Since he learned the "husband" rules primarily from observing his father's treatment of his mother, he learned that husbands save money by eating at home. Had he been reared by a father who had continued to court his wife after marriage, he would probably recognize the value of continued romantic dinners at fine restaurants.

The intent of courtship is not merely to "land a partner" but to perpetuate feelings of affection. The most important issue is not that you and your partner *got married* but whether the two of you still *want to be married.* Failure to recognize the need for lifelong courtship often leads to divorce. Love "cannot be expected to last forever unless it is continually fed with portions of love, the manifestation of esteem and admiration, the expressions of gratitude, and the consideration of unselfishness."[3]

Failure to continue to court one another may tip the scales toward divorce. Divorce usually represents not just an emotional setback for both partners but a financial setback as well. In fact, for most divorced people divorce is *the* most expensive event—both financially and emotionally—that will ever happen to them. As we grow up, we develop a timetable of when we believe certain events are supposed to take place and in what sequence. This "schedule" provides us a general guideline for where we should be in life at a given age. Traumatic events such as divorce tend to throw us off track and make us feel we are "behind schedule" in the life cycle. But life operates on its own schedule, and although anticipated timetables are disrupted when divorce unexpectedly returns married people to single life, most will remarry and continue life with a modified schedule.

Married or Single, with Children Ages 1–9

The primary financial tasks associated with this phase of Stage 2 are to provide for the costs of childbearing and child rearing. Having adequate medical insurance coverage is essential in order to avoid a financial catastrophe should complications arise from the births of the children. As the size of the family increases, the need for a larger place to live also increases, and the need to buy a home often becomes a major goal. However, if the young family has already overextended its credit, qualifying for a loan, let alone saving for a down payment, may be difficult. These tasks are made even more difficult by the need to adjust to the income of only one wage earner as the new mother settles into her maternal role. In addition to meeting the challenging needs of a growing family, young families must set short- and long-term goals, such as accumulating educational funds for the children, buying life insurance, and making out a will with guardianship instructions.

As all parents know, rearing children is an expensive undertaking. It is estimated that for a middle-income family, the average annual cost of rearing an elementary school-age child in the United States is about $8,000. It costs about $148,000 to rear one child over a seventeen-year period. Since children can share resources, each additional child does not represent an exact multiple of the cost of rearing one child. However, the cost of rearing one daughter is $25,000 more than the cost of rearing a son. A family can expect to devote 75 percent of its projected real income to the cost of rearing children. If a couple without children were to invest the amount of money it costs to rear and educate two children, they could retire and live for the rest of their lives on the $40,000 a year they would earn from just the *interest* on that investment!

Many of us have heard the counsel, "Have fun while you can, because once the children come along, it's just hard work and debt." If we hear this kind of thing repeatedly while we're growing up, it can become part of the rules that govern how we think and act as adults. After we have children, we may become preoccupied with working to provide for the family and not have as much time for our spouse. We may even feel ill prepared for the job of being parents, and overwhelmed by the ever-increasing costs of rearing children.

If you have received from your family of origin the message that mothers and fathers are supposed to sacrifice themselves for the sake of their children, you may feel guilty taking time or money for your own needs. Think about how things might change if you were to teach your children that parents are people too, and that they do not relinquish their right to happiness just because they have had children.

Stage 3: Married or Single, with Children Ages 10–19

Everyday life and family finances become more complex at this stage. As children grow and change, family rules governing their behavior must also change. The rules governing a twelve-year-old are most likely different from those governing a six-year-old. This applies to money matters as well. Parents begin to extend or restrict money limits as children become able to handle the financial responsibilities of growing up. The need to include financial limits and rules is essential to teaching children about money management; otherwise, overindulgence may give them a false impression of what it's like to live in the real world. Parents must increase their income and set limits on their own spending because the costs of rearing teenagers will dwarf the cost of rearing children under the age of twelve. In addition, major household appliances begin to wear out, college tuition looms in the not-too-distant future, and thoughts of retirement needs begin to surface.

If your children are caught up in the latest fads and are basing their self-esteem on how much money is spent on them, review chapter 3's recommendations. Building bonds of love through spending time together and treating each other with respect and affection will be far easier on your budget than trying with money to satisfy insatiable desires for things.

When Children Become Teenagers

The transition from having elementary school-age children to having teenage children can be particularly difficult. One parent commented, "I wonder why they call them *teen*agers when it would be more accurate to call them *parent*agers." This kind of remark stems from the emotional and financial changes families undergo during this stage of the life cycle. As the financial demands of the family escalate, many families employ the rob-Peter-to-pay-Paul method of managing finances, juggling investment and retirement money in order to meet current demands.

This stage requires an increase in almost all categories of the family budget, especially the entertainment/recreation portion. Teenagers' transportation costs are eight times greater than those of third-graders, and their food consumption is three times greater.[4] Money previously budgeted for running the household often no longer stretches to the end of the month. Food budgets that had been sufficient for years become woefully inadequate. Unfortunately, the spouse who is responsible for household expenditures will often be accused of mismanagement by an unsympathetic partner, and unfair comparisons are sometimes made with families of equal size but with younger children.

Remember that each family is different, and that parents usually approach teenage issues based on rules that governed them as teenagers. Differences in approach can lead to conflicts over who is being "too soft" or "too hard" on the child. One way of resolving such differences is to implement a cost-sharing practice such as a *fifty/fifty agreement.*

A fifty/fifty agreement can help to encourage mutual consideration for each other's feelings, increase the level of cooperation, and broaden a sense of appreciation for assets. A fifty/fifty agreement states that parents will pay half the cost of an item if the child will pay the other half—a dollar-for-dollar matching agreement. Under such an agreement, the child is more able to accumulate enough money to buy items, must put forth effort and sacrifice to obtain money, and has the opportunity not only to learn the benefits of cooperating with others but also to appreciate the efforts and generosity of others.

Remember that people cooperate most effectively when each sees the other as an equal and when dominance and submission are *reciprocal roles of responsibility* rather than positions of superiority and inferiority.

Stage 4: Married or Single, Launching Children

When a child leaves home, the change can be hard on everyone involved. Yet most parents know from the beginning that their primary purpose is to prepare their children to become independent and able to succeed on their own. A universal family rule is "Sooner or later, the child must go." The only question is, "When and under what circumstances will the launch take place?"

No longer having to take care of children, however, is often replaced with having to take care of parents. As a consequence, getting rid of the big house may be postponed, and finances that had been earmarked for retirement may have to be diverted. The need to help pay bills for adult children may place an added burden on the family budget.

Launching Adult Children

Until recently, children were expected to leave home upon reaching adulthood or sooner. Back in sixteenth-century England, many children left home for school or apprenticeships at the age of six or seven.[5] In France, seven- and eight-year-old children left home to work as servants, and Swiss children of similar age went to work for weavers.[6] During the seventeenth century, children frequently left home between ten and fifteen.[7]

The appropriate launching age can vary greatly depending on social norms. For example, one parent may believe that a child of eighteen is too young to leave home but that a child approaching twenty-five is way past due. Another parent's rules might dictate that children leave home at twenty-two unless they are attending college. A child may be considered too young to get married at one age and yet be pressured into getting married at another age. However, as you may have already observed, just because children get married does not mean that they will not be coming back home to live.

Failure to Launch

One reason today's children leave home at an older age is finances. The 1970s and 1980s offered extensive financial growth to "baby boom" parents. Their success enabled them to provide a setting that is difficult for their children to duplicate. As a result, their children may be somewhat reluctant to leave the comfortable, parent-financed environment for a less comfortable, self-financed one. "I have it pretty good here at home," they may think. "Nice house, car, laundry service, good food—and I don't have to pay for it. Why in the world would I want to leave?" One of the problems with this perspective is that many parents look forward to life after their children leave home!

Adult children stay at home for other reasons. For one thing, when marriages fail, the children sometimes feel obligated to fulfill their parents' emotional needs. The parents develop an emotional dependence on their children while the children maintain their financial dependence on their parents. They each begin to believe they cannot make it on their own, so they fail to develop self-confidence and self-reliance.

Occasionally, families have an implicit rule that a child is *not* to leave home but is to stay with or near the parents. While they may not verbalize such a rule, siblings seem to know which one of them has inherited the primary responsibility for taking care of the parents. The rest of the children are free to marry and move to whatever part of the country they wish—unless, of course, family rules tell them not to live too far away.

Sometimes the designated caretaker is allowed to marry but not to move far away, or is allowed to marry but must keep the parents at the top of the priority list. These rules may conflict with the family rules of the caretaker's spouse—rules that may admonish children to leave their father and mother, set up their own household, and place top priority on the spouse.

Delayed launching or lack of launching—regardless of the reason—can have far-reaching financial implications for the parents. In previous decades, married couples tended to have their children during their late teens or early twenties. Most of these children left home when they were eighteen or twenty and when their parents were in their late thirties or early forties. This left parents about twenty-five years to prepare for retirement.

Many of today's married couples—who do not even marry until their mid-twenties—do not have children until their *late* twenties or early thirties. If their children do not leave home until the children's late twenties, the parents' time—and funds—to prepare for retirement can be cut to fewer than ten years. In addition, parents often face the substantial costs of maintaining or financially helping adult children (those who still live at home as well as those who have moved out) with money that could go to retirement needs.

The Launching Fund

Some families' rules dictate that children should be provided for until they leave home at a certain age. After that, children should be able to make it on their own. Some parents require that adult children cover their own living expenses, though the parents may allow their children to use an old car until the children can afford to buy one for themselves. Some parents provide a *launching fund* to help their children reach a state of self-reliance.

A launching fund helps children leaving home make the transition from financial dependence on their parents to financial independence. For example, a launching fund might help pay for a child's rent over a five-month period. During the first month, the parents pay all the rent. During the second month, they pay 75 percent of the rent. The third month, the parents pay half the rent. The fourth month, they pay 25 percent. By the fifth month, the child pays all the rent. A progressively less-supportive fund helps children feel less "kicked out," and helps parents feel that they are helping their children move into the adult world.

Launching funds can help pay for college, vocational training, a new business, moving costs and rent, or the down payment on a home. These funds can also be used to relaunch adult children who have returned home due to loss of employment, divorce, illness, or other challenges. You can set whatever conditions, restrictions, and guidelines you feel comfortable with to govern the fund's use.

The launching fund can be paid into by the parents alone, by pre-determined contributions from all family members, or through a pay-back agreement whereby each person who uses the fund agrees to reimburse it in a timely and responsible manner. Children who break the rules forfeit privileges to use the fund. After the children are all launched, any remaining money will be available for the parents.

Stage 5: Married or Single, with Children Launched

As the number of people living at home decreases, income is divided among fewer individuals, and the economic well-being of the remaining family increases. When all children have been successfully launched, the income is divided between only two people. Dreams and goals that were put off until the children were on their own can finally be realized. For many couples, this opportunity comes just in time, because their income typically starts to decrease at this stage of the life cycle.

The "empty nest syndrome" once described parents who were depressed and devoid of meaning in their lives. This does not seem to be the case in today's families. An ever-increasing number of parents who have launched their children now launch themselves into meaningful and fulfilling endeavors. "Empty nest, full life" is a more accurate description of people in this situation.

Couples are likely to grow individually and in their marriage relationship during this period. Husbands and wives once again become top priorities in each other's lives. They can concentrate more on their own lives and outside interests than was possible while they were rearing children.

Stage 6: Married or Single, Retired

It is estimated that by 2025 almost one in every five Americans will be sixty-five or older,[8] and the vast majority of these people will be retired. For many of us, the dream of retirement includes being independent enough to do what we want, adventurous and healthy enough to go where we want, and financially secure enough to realize both. But such is not always the case. To many, retirement is either a time to enjoy the "good life" or a time to struggle on a fixed income.

Living standards usually have to be adjusted downward after retirement, while reliance on community and government resources has to be adjusted upward. Many discover too late that they did not adequately finance unexpected medical costs, leisure activities, and travel. Concerns focus on how much of a nest egg they have, how long it might last, and what to do with what is left over (estate planning). Those in line for an inheritance are often concerned about how to reduce probate costs, and about how their elderly parents will spend their money and whether they will be victimized by a scam artist.

How Long Will You Live?

One of the unique challenges associated with financial planning for retirement is estimating how long you will live. During the first half of this century, longevity was not an issue because the average worker was not expected to reach the retirement age of 65. The life expectancy for females was 65.4 in 1940, but the life expectancy for males did not reach 65 until 1950. By 1990, the life expectancy for females had risen to 78 and for males to 72.

To estimate more accurately your life expectancy, you may wish to complete Worksheet 11.1, How Long Will You Live? (page 209).

How Much Income Will You Need?

For the elderly, as well as for other age groups, a sense of satisfaction depends on more than just personal income.[9] Many people with low incomes are quite satisfied with their lives, while some with high incomes are dissatisfied. Satisfaction largely depends on the concept of *relative deprivation*.[10] Relative deprivation is an interpretation of your well-being compared to that of your friends and neighbors. You can have a low income but be better off than those around you and feel fairly satisfied. Conversely, if you have a fairly high income but the incomes of those around you are higher, you could feel dissatisfied.

The amount of income you will need in retirement depends largely on the standard of living you wish to maintain. The U.S. Department of Labor estimates that a retired couple needs 65 to 80 percent of their preretirement income to maintain their current standard of living.[11]

Wills and Estate Transfer

A will enables you to transfer your property to others after your death. A will should do the following:

1. Revoke previous wills.

2. Identify members of your family.

3. Appoint a personal representative.

4. Identify debts and estate taxes.

5. Provide instructions regarding the distribution of personal belongings.

6. Explain which responsibilities the spouse should assume.

7. Explain how all other responsibilities should be distributed.

8. Include a common disaster clause: what to do if both spouses die simultaneously.

9. Give authority to others to help the spouse deal with taxes and complicated business transactions.

10. Describe the scope of the will and any property pertaining thereto.

11. Define terms such as *children.* (Does *children* refer to all descendants, natural children, adopted children?)

12. Include a severability clause. (If part of the will is unenforceable, the rest is still valid.)

13. Specify whether inheritances are to be divided among grandchildren on a per-capita basis or on the basis of their parent's share.

14. Appoint guardians for dependent children.

15. Provide "living will" instructions and answer life-support questions.

If you should die *intestate*—that is, without a will—your state's intestate laws will distribute the resources of your estate as prescribed in the state code. A will, however, does not avoid *probate*—the legal process by which the state transfers property. Property referred to in a will is still subject to probate. You can avoid probate for your heirs, saving them time and money, if you make arrangements for your property to be transferred automatically upon your death. Such a transfer can take place in three ways: *joint ownership, incomplete transfers,* and *revocable living trusts.*

Joint ownership. A couple owns real estate jointly if each partner is listed as a joint tenant, cars are owned jointly if both names appear on the title, and bank accounts are considered joint if both names appear on them.

Incomplete transfers. In an incomplete transfer, you transfer property to a child, but you retain the right to revoke the transfer. For example, you might transfer ownership of your home to your child, with the understanding that you will live there rent free until you die. It is a legal and literal transfer, and your child must pay the taxes. But the right to revoke the transfer provides protection against unscrupulous offspring who might decide they need the equity in your house more than you do and try to sell the property before you finish using it. An incomplete transfer is revocable as long as you are alive; however, upon your death the property automatically transfers to whoever has been named on the deed.

Revocable living trust. A revocable living trust functions like an incomplete transfer, but it applies to assets other than real estate. You set up a revocable living trust prior to your death. In your will, you include details identifying assets and the trustee who will act as executor. When you use a revocable living trust, you still have to pay taxes on the property while you are living, but upon your death the trust will automatically transfer.

NOTES

1. American Council on Life Insurance, 1970.
2. U.S. Department of Commerce, 1996.
3. Kimball, 1980, 8.
4. Facing up to the high cost of kids, 1983.
5. Illick, 1974.
6. Shorter, 1975.
7. Illick, 1974; Wall, 1978.
8. Euzeby, 1989.
9. Russell, 1990.
10. Liang and Doherty, 1980; Liang and Fairchild, 1979.
11. U.S. Department of Labor, 1989.

WORKSHEET 11.1—HOW LONG WILL YOU LIVE?

Start with the number 72.

Personal Facts

If you are male, subtract 3.

If you are female, add 4.

If you live in an urban area with a population over 2 million, subtract 2.

If you live in a town under 10,000 or on a farm, add 2.

If any grandparent lived to 85, add 2.

If all four grandparents lived to 80, add 6.

If either parent died of a stroke or heart attack before age 50, subtract 4.

If any parent, brother, or sister under 50 has (or had) cancer or a heart condition, or has had diabetes since childhood, subtract 3.

If you earn at least $50,000 a year, subtract 2.

If you finished college, add 1. If you have a graduate or professional degree, add 2 more.

If you are 65 or over and are still working, add 3.

If you live with a spouse or friend, add 5. If not, subtract 1 for every ten years alone since age 25.

Lifestyle Status

If you work behind a desk, subtract 3.

If your work requires regular, heavy physical labor, add 3.

If you exercise strenuously five times a week for at least half an hour, add 4. If two or three times a week, add 2.

If you sleep more than ten hours each night, subtract 4.

If you are intense, aggressive, or easily angered, subtract 3.

If you are easygoing and relaxed, add 3.

If you are happy, add 1; if unhappy, subtract 2.

If you have had a speeding ticket in the past year, subtract 1.

If you smoke more than two packs of cigarettes a day, subtract 8; if one to two packs, subtract 6; if half to one, subtract 3.

If you drink the equivalent of one and one-half ounces of liquor a day, subtract 1.

If you are overweight by 50 pounds or more, subtract 8; if by 30 to 50 pounds, subtract 4; if by 10 to 30 pounds, subtract 2.

If you are a man over 40 and have annual checkups, add 2.

If you are a woman and see a gynecologist once a year, add 2.

Running Total _____

Age Adjustment
If you are between 30 and 40, add 2.
If you are between 40 and 50, add 3.
If you are between 50 and 70, add 4.
If you are over 70, add 5.

Add up your score to arrive at your life expectancy.

Total (Your Life Expectancy) _____

From: Robert R. Allen with Shirley Linde, *Lifegain*, 1981, Englewood Cliffs, New Jersey: Appleton Books.

APPENDIX

The Ten Financial Principles

Principle 1: Financial problems are usually behavior problems rather than money problems.

Principle 2: If you continue doing what you have been doing, you will continue getting what you have been getting.

Principle 3: Nothing (no thing) is worth risking the relationship.

Principle 4: Money spent on things you value usually leads to a feeling of satisfaction and accomplishment. Money spent on things you do not value usually leads to a feeling of frustration and futility.

Principle 5: We know the price of everything and the value of nothing.

Principle 6: You can never get enough of what you don't need, because what you don't need can never satisfy you.

Principle 7: Financial freedom is more often the result of decreased spending than of increased income.

Principle 8: Be grateful for what you have.

Principle 9: The best things in life are free.

Principle 10: The value of individuals should never be equated with their net worth.

REFERENCES

Adler, A. (1927). *The Practice and Theory of Individual Psychology.* New York: Harcourt, Brace and World.

Allen, R. R., and Linde, S. (1981). *Lifegain.* Englewood Cliffs, New Jersey: Appleton Books.

American Council on Life Insurance. (1970). *Adult Financial Management Matrix.* Poster, 1850 K Street, N.W., Washington, D.C.

Aquinas, T. (1952). "Summa Theologica." In *Saint Thomas Aquinas, Great Books of the Western World.* New York: Encyclopedia Britannica, Inc.

Aristotle (1952). "Politics." In *Aristotle, Great Books of the Western World.* New York: Encyclopedia Britannica.

Ashton, M. J. (1975). "One for the Money." *Ensign,* July:72–73.

Benenson, H. (1984). "Women's Occupational and Family Achievement in the U.S." *British Journal of Sociology,* 35:19–41.

Berardo, D. H., Sherhan, C. L., and Leslie, G. R. (1987). "A Residue of Tradition: Jobs, Careers, and Spouses' Time in Housework." *Journal of Marriage and the Family,* 49:381–90.

Berger, P. K., and Ivancevich, J. M. (1973). "Birth Order and Managerial Achievement." *Academy of Management Journal,* 16:515–19.

Bernard, H., and Huckins, W. (1975). *Dynamics of Personal Adjustment.* Boston: Holbrook Press.

Canner, G., and Cyrnak, A. W. (1985). "Recent Developments in Credit Card Holding and Use Patterns among U.S. Families." *Journal of Retail Banking,* 3:63–73.

Coleman, M., and Ganong, L. N. (1985). "Remarriage Myths: Implications for the Helping Professions." *Journal of Counseling and Development,* 64:116-20.

D'Amico, R. (1983). "Status Maintenance or Status Competition? Wife's Relative Wages as a Determinant of Labor Supply and Marital Instability." *Social Forces*, 61:1186–1205.

Euzeby, C. (1989). "Noncontributory Old Age Pensions: A Possible Solution in OECD Countries." *International Labor Review*, 128:11–28.

Edmondson, M. E., and Pasley, K. (1986). "Financial Counseling Attitudes and Interests: An Exploratory Study of Remarried Individuals." In K. Kitt (ed.), *Quality Control in an Emerging Profession: Proceedings of the Association for Financial Counseling and Planning Educators Annual Conference* (1–10). Austin, Texas: University of Texas, University Press.

"Facing Up to the High Cost of Kids." (1983). *Changing Times*, April:28–31.

Foa, U. (1971). "Interpersonal and Economic Resources." *Science*, 29 January:345–51.

Freud, S. (1913). "On Beginning the Treatment." In J. Strachey (ed. and trans.), *The Standard Edition of the Complete Psychological Works of Sigmund Freud.* (Vol. 1). London: Hogarth Press.

Fromm, E. (1955). *The Sane Society.* New York: Holt, Rinehart.

Galligan, R., and Bahr, S. (1978). "Economic Well-Being and Marital Stability: Implications for Income Maintenance Programs." *Journal of Marriage and the Family*, 40:283–90.

General Mills. (1975). *The General Mills American Family Report, 1974–75; A Study of the American Family and Money.* Minneapolis: General Mills.

Hanson, S. L. (1991). "The Economic Costs and Rewards of Two-Earner, Two-Parent Families. *Journal of Marriage and the Family*, 53:622–34.

Heath, D. (1986). *America in Perspective.* Boston: Houghton Mifflin.

Henley, W. E. (1978). "Invictus." In S. Honor and T. Hunt, *Philosophy.* Belmont, California: Wadsworth.

Hogan, J., and Bauer, J. (1988). "Problems in Family Financial Management." In C. S. Chilman, F. M. Cox, and E. W. Nunnally (eds.), *Employment and Economic Problems* (137–53). Beverly Hills, California: Sage Publications.

Holmes, O. W. (1858). *The Autocrat of the Breakfast Table.* Boston: Phillips, Sampson, and Company.

Hudson, V. (1900). "Birth Order of World Leaders: An Exploratory Analysis of Effects on Personality and Behavior." *Political Psychology*, 11:583-601.

Ihinger-Tallman, M., and Pasley, K. (1981). *Factors Influencing Stability in Remarriage.* Paper presented at the annual meetings of the International Sociological Association, Leuven, Belgium.

Ilfeld, F. W. (1982). "Marital Stressors, Coping Styles, and Symptoms of Depression." In L. Goldberger and S. Bregnitz (eds.), *Handbook of Stress* (303–50). New York: Psychohistory Press.

Illick, J. E. (1974). "Children in Seventeenth Century England and America." In L. de Mause (Ed.), *The History of Childhood* (303–50). New York: Psychohistory Press.

James, W. (1956). *The Will to Believe.* New York: Dover.

Kimball, S. W. (1980). *Marriage.* Salt Lake City: Deseret Book.

———. (1982). *Teachings of Spencer W. Kimball.* Salt Lake City: Bookcraft.

Kohlberg, L. (1963). "The Development of Children's Orientations Toward a Moral Order: Sequence in the Development of Moral Thought." *Vita Humana*, 6:11–33.

———. (1969). "Stages and Sequence: The Cognitive-Developmental Approach to Socialization." In C. A. Goslin (ed.), *Handbook of Socialization Theory and Research* (374–80). Chicago: Rand McNally.

Krueger, D. (1986). *The Last Taboo.* New York: Brunner/Mazel.

Liang, J., and Doherty, E. (1980). "Financial Well-Being among the Aged: A Further Elaboration." *Journal of Gerontology*, 35:409–20.

Liang, J., and Fairchild, T. J. (1979). "Relative Deprivation and Perception of Financial Adequacy among the Aged." *Journal of Gerontology*, 34:746–59.

McCrae, S. (1987). "Allocation of Money in Cross-Class Families." *Sociological Review*, 35:97–122.

Milton, John (1996). *Paradise Lost.* ed. Harold Bloom. New York: Chelsea House.

Moore, K., and Hofferth, S. (1979). "Effects of Women's Employment on Marriage: Formation, Stability, and Roles." In *Marriage and Family Review*, 2:27–36.

Mueller, M. J., and Hira, T. K. (1984). "Impact of Money Management Practices on Household Solvency Status." In K. P. Goebel (ed.), *Proceedings of the American Council on Consumer Interests Annual Conference* (76–79). Columbia, Missouri: University of Missouri Press.

Nye, F. I., and Hoffman, L. W. (1974). *Working Mothers.* San Francisco: Jossey-Bass.

Orthner, D. (1990). "Parental Work and Early Adolescence: Issues for Research and Practice." *Journal of Early Adolescence*, 10:246–59.

Pahl, J. (1983). "The Allocation of Money and the Structuring of Inequality within Marriage." *Sociological Review*, 31:237–62.

————. (1990). "Household Spending, Personal Spending, and the Control of Money in Marriage." *Sociology*, 24:119–38.

Pasley, K. (1987). "Family Boundary Ambiguity: Perceptions of Adult Remarried Family Members." In K. Pasley and M. Ihinger-Tallman (Eds.), *Remarriage and Stepparenting: Current Research and Theory* (206–24). New York: Guilford Press.

Peck, M. S. (1978). *The Road Less Traveled.* New York: Touchstone Book.

Poduska, B. E. (1989). "Crisis Counseling." *Journal of Financial Planning*, 2:114–19.

Poduska, B. E., and Allred, G. H. (1987). *Personal Financial Management and Birth Order.* Unpublished manuscript, Brigham Young University, Provo, Utah.

Price-Bonham, S., and Murphy, D. C. (1980). "Dual-Career Marriages: Implications for the Clinician." *Journal of Marital and Family Therapy*, 6:181–88.

Rapoport, R., and Rapoport, R. (1971). "The Dual-Career Family: A Variant Pattern and Social Change." In C. Safilios-Rothschild (ed.), *Toward a Sociology of Women* (128–47), Lexington, Massachusetts: Xerox.

————. (1976). *Dual-Career Families Reexamined.* New York: Harper and Row.

Rejda, G. (1982). *Principles of Insurance.* London: Scott, Foresman and Company.

Russell, R. (1990). "Recreation and Quality of Life in Old Age." *Journal of Applied Gerontology*, 9:77–90.

Schaninger, C. M., and Buss, W. C. (1986). "A Longitudinal Comparison of Consumption and Finance Handling between Happily Married and Divorced Couples." *Journal of Marriage and the Family*, 48:129–36.

Shorter, E. (1975). *The Making of the Modern Family.* New York: Basic Books.

Smith, R. E. (1979). *The Subtle Revolution: Women at Work.* Washington, D.C.: Urban Institute.

South, S., and Spitze, G. (1986). "Determinants of Divorce over the Marital Life Course." *American Sociological Review*, 51:583–90.

Spitze, G., and South, S. (1985). "Women's Employment, Time Expenditure, and Divorce." *Journal of Family Issues*, 8:307–29.

Steggell, G. L., Allred, G. H., Harper, J. M., and Poduska, B. E. (1990). *Influence of Spouses' Birth Order on Couples' Income and Expenditure Patterns.* Unpublished dissertation, Brigham Young University, Provo, Utah.

Thomas, S., Albrecht, K., and White, P. (1984). "Determinants of Marital Quality in Dual-Career Couples." *Family Relations*, 33:513–21.

U.S. Department of Commerce. (1990a). *Statistical Abstract of the United States*, 1990. Washington, D.C.: U.S. Government Printing Office.

———. (1994, 1994b, 1994c). *Statistical Abstract of the United States, 1994.* Washington, D.C.: U.S. Government Printing Office.

U. S. Department of Commerce, Bureau of Economic Analysis. (1990b). *The National Income and Product Accounts of the United States, 1929–82.* Washington, D.C.: U.S. Government Printing Office.

U. S. Department of Health and Human Services. (1990). *Alcohol and Health. Special Report to the U.S. Congress.* Washington, D.C.: U.S. Government Printing Office.

U. S. Department of Labor, Bureau of Labor Statistics. (1989). *Monthly Labor Review,* 112:37–41.

Wilhelm, M. S., Iams, D. R., and Ridley, C. A. (1987). "Unemployment and Marital Well-Being: The Impact of Changes in Financial Management." In M. Edmondson and L. Perch (eds.), *Accenting our Focus on Competing Professional Enrichment: Proceedings of the Association for Financial Counseling and Planning Educators Annual Conference.* Lexington, Kentucky: University of Kentucky, University Press.

Watzlawick, P., Weakland, J., and Fisch, R. (1974). *Change: Principles of Problem Formation and Problem Resolution.* New York: Norton.

Yeh, B., and Lester, D. (1987). "Statewide Divorce Rates and Wives' Participation in the Labor Market." *Journal of Divorce,* 11:107–14.

———. (1988). "Wives Who Work Full-Time and Part-Time: Correlates Over the States of the U.S.A." *Psychological Reports,* 62:545–46.

Young, B. (1864). *Journal of Discourses,* 26 vols. (London: Latter-day Saints' Book Depot, 1854–86), 10:329.

INDEX